contemporary
indian cuisine

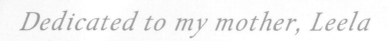

Dedicated to my mother, Leela

contemporary
indian cuisine

anil ashokan

photography by greg elms

First published in the UK in 2008 by
Apple Press
7 Greenland Street
London NW1 0ND
United Kingdom
www.apple-press.com

First published in Australia in 2008 by
Allen & Unwin
83 Alexander Street
Crows Nest NSW 2065
Australia
Phone: (61 2) 8425 0100
Fax: (61 2) 9906 2218
Email: info@allenandunwin.com
Web: www.allenandunwin.com

ISBN 978-1-84543-262-1

Photography by Greg Elms
Food styled by Virginia Dowzer
Edited by Susin Chow
Indexed by Trevor Matthews
Text designed and typeset by Nada Backovic Designs
Printed and bound in Malaysia

Our thanks to Empire 111 for the generous loan of the crockery used in the photography.

10 9 8 7 6 5 4 3 2 1

WORCESTERSHIRE COUNTY COUNCIL	
098	
Bertrams	19.04.08
641.5954	£14.99
KD	

Contents

THE FRESH APPROACH

indian cuisine:
the Qmin perspective

After love there is only cuisine.

CHARLIE TROTTER

Food is central to Indian culture. It's an integral part of daily life and dominates much of our conversation.

Like all other old-world cuisines, Indian cuisine has had an interesting evolution. What began as home cooking became different regional 'styles' that were then influenced to different extents by traders and invaders like the French, British, Dutch, Portuguese, Arabs, Persians and Chinese. Taste, colour and texture are determined by the available ingredients of the region, and this can vary enormously within the space of a few kilometres.

Today when I am asked to describe the nature of Indian cuisine, I find it most useful to simply compare it to European cuisine: its variety as contrasting from region to region as, say, French is to German or Spanish to Italian.

One of the biggest challenges in compiling a collection like this is that on the whole, traditional recipes have never been written down. Family secrets, special tricks, closely held traditions and beliefs have meant recipes and methodologies have not been precisely documented so universal standards are often vague. Fortunately there are some fundamental rules to the preparation of most classical dishes. For example, the internationally famous North Indian dish 'Butter chicken' always has tomato and would never have creamed corn as the base.

What's more, because masters of the art avoided recording their works for fear of losing their secrets, as a cuisine it is largely misunderstood and misinterpreted outside the country. The words 'hot', 'spicy' and 'curry' are used the world over in relation to Indian food; the words 'pungent' and 'aromatic' less so, though they are probably more appropriate. But times are changing.

For centuries cooking methods have involved a long list of ingredients and hours of intensive labour to produce a meal—both things that the modern cook lacks. My aim is to maintain the authenticity of traditional flavours without having to resort to shortcuts like boiling up curry powders. I like to promote new techniques, products and appliances to simplify the process and I always encourage exploration and experimentation with the best and freshest ingredients available.

I believe that looking back at the evolution of this cuisine is intrinsic to understanding it. I also believe in furthering that evolution.

Over the years I have arrived at the idea of representing certain dishes in a set style by combining a number of different interpretations, with an eye to simplifying preparation and enhancing flexibility. With this in mind I have included tips and special notes suggesting you try different flavours, using your own local produce or perhaps healthier alternative ingredients.

Although a meal may comprise several recipes on one plate, I would never suggest cooking a North Indian fish and smothering it with, say, a South Indian style sauce. So please do not mistake this as 'fusion' food. All the recipes are based on authentic ingredients for the cuisine without introducing any foreign influences. However, I may suggest a more locally available fish, or an easier or more accessible cooking method.

For me, one of the greatest pleasures in cooking is to express yourself in the dish, to find your creativity and sensuality in the choices you make and the way you prepare it. Use this book as an inspirational starting point or a step-by-step guide—it's up to you!

evolution of my approach

Born into a working-class family in an average Bombay suburb, I had no official links with the culinary world. Yet my mother was truly one of my greatest inspirations. With limited resources she turned out the most wonderful meals on her little kerosene-fired

stove when I was a child. It was here that she taught me that cooking is about caring, and the gratitude from those who enjoy it is your reward.

My father, too, must take some credit, because it was he who insisted that we be open-minded about food, that we try all forms of fish, meat, offal, and anything else that came our way, even though at home we ate only vegetarian food.

There are a host of friends who have helped me along the way, in particular three who enrolled with me at the Bombay hospitality school. Each of us aspired to become a professional chef—all four succeeded, and three of us still are!

My first permanent job upon graduation was at the Taj Mahal Hotel. Entering the Taj kitchens as a new trainee was like being flung into the bear pit. It was ruled over by Satish Arora and his tight-knit team of sous chefs, and they kept us scurrying. In the first two months it seemed so tough I was ready to hang up my apron, but it turned out to be incredible training in all aspects of food production.

After a year, I was sent to a number of premium properties in the hotel chain and worked alongside some of the best exponents of Indian food. Among them, Chef Arvind Saraswat and his extremely talented team of sous chefs in Delhi put us through rigorous exercises including banqueting and top-class Indian dining, developing skills that I use to this day.

I made many friends during that time, several of them senior chefs running their own kitchens who shared their experiences and family traditions with me. I also travelled extensively internationally and took invaluable lessons from different cultures: the precision of the Swiss, the discipline of the Japanese, the passion of the French, and the creativity of the Singaporeans, to name but a few.

In the mid-1980s one of the Taj's most enthusiastic customers was an Australian businessman and self-confessed Indophile. Every time Ed Gabriel visited, he would urge me to move to Sydney and open a top-notch Indian restaurant where I could showcase my work. The time was not yet right, but a dream was born ...

In the meantime I met Chef Prem Kumar who was then deputed to the London operations of the Taj. Along with Ms Camellia Punjabi (the VP of the hotel group), he developed an approach to cooking that has been fundamental to my career. They taught me to look for the details of the cuisine—the background, the history, the compositions, the motives behind the compositions—and a whole new world opened up.

In 1989 the concept of opening a restaurant in Sydney was coming together. While Ed was working hard on setting it up (sadly a professional partnership never eventuated), I moved to Australia and began working in various establishments around Sydney. I learnt as much about what not to do as what to do!

Among these experiences I spent two years as sous chef to Stephen Tryon, a chef from one of the Michelin star restaurants in London, who taught me a great deal about the way these places attain such a high standard. Not only did he encourage me to source and use the freshest of local produce and to forge relationships with my suppliers, but he also showed me how to set up and run an effective kitchen team.

Then an amazing opportunity came my way. For over six years I worked in a five-star hotel as assistant to Executive Chef Jacky Ternisien, who generously shared decades of global experience with me. It was a challenge being responsible for the operation of several kitchens and an army of chefs and apprentices, but the excellent facilities, top-quality ingredients and a highly supportive management team allowed me to create and experiment with different menus for fine-dining restaurants, bistros, room service, pub fare and huge banquets at the same time.

The work of Tetsuya Wakuda and Neil Perry was particularly influential during this time and discovering the cookbooks of Charlie Trotter had an enormous impact. When my wife and I took an extended trip through the eateries and restaurants of Europe and the US, a meal at Trotter's in Chicago was a highlight.

I returned to Sydney brimming with inspiration and determined to share my life's work by offering a unique restaurant experience. Starting small, I ran a brasserie at a hotel complex and with help from the owner (Mr Ervin Vidor) and his family, we traded for over six successful years.

Next I progressed to a small restaurant I named Kokum (a popular Indian spice) specialising in Portuguese-influenced dishes from Goa. The food was excellent and its authenticity attracted legions of customers and great responses from the food media. Even more flattering was the fact that seven new Goan restaurants sprang up in Sydney over the next three years!

Unfortunately, the business side of things did not go so well. The demise of Kokum taught me some hard lessons, but somehow with the unconditional love and support of my family, I managed to pick myself up and start again. This time I had to start from scratch—designing and building from the ground up—but in January 2004 Qmin finally opened its doors.

The venue is stunning and my team is formidable. We have exemplary Indian chefs and my good friend Andy Bantock fronted the service crew.

As I reflect on my journey and launch into my latest venture, the Qmin cookbook, the words of Johann Wolfgang von Goethe (quoted in Charlie Trotter's first book) linger in my mind:

> *Whatever you can do or dream you can, begin it. Boldness has genius, power, and magic in it. Begin it now!*

about the recipes

Enjoy the warmth—not just the heat!

QMIN SAYING

So many Indian cookbooks rely on attractive props to make their food look appealing. I have always believed that good food carefully presented will speak for itself.

At Qmin we have devised a concept called 'Maharaja's Table' that presents Indian food in the style of a degustation menu. We base each menu on a different dynasty of kings, researching them all in great detail. Every dish is individually plated in a modern style and accompanied by a carefully chosen beverage. The concept has been a huge success and you can see the results as they form the basis of some photographs in this book. I urge you to mix and match the different dishes.

There are notes accompanying all the recipes for marinades, relishes, chutneys and breads that encourage you to use them with different dishes, or even as the basis of a meal.

All of these recipes have been made over and over again for accuracy, and tested by professional chefs. I have found that variations in the result are primarily due to three factors.

The first is timing. Spices are extremely delicate and the duration of cooking can alter their flavour dramatically. Second, substituting local produce in place of the listed ingredients will, of course, make a difference. And third, the quantities of salt (or any other spice mix containing salt), sour (by which I mean ingredients like tomatoes, tamarind, yoghurt and lemon juice) and chilli heat (fresh or dry in any form), are crucial to the character of the final dish. Even the sequence in which they are added to the cooking can alter the outcome.

In the interests of simplicity, I will sometimes suggest alternative cooking techniques. Not every kitchen has a 'tandoor' (Indian clay oven), for example, but a grill, griddle or conventional oven will perform just as well in most cases.

As a general rule, I use refined vegetable oil in my recipes. You may prefer another neutral oil of your choice, but be aware that the flavour will alter slightly. To keep fat content down, quantities of oil, ghee and butter have been slightly reduced from the original. If you wish to cut down even more, in most slow-cooked dishes the oil will eventually separate so it can be skimmed off altogether.

I would always recommend that you keep the oil that has been removed because it is infused with the flavour and aroma of the spices in the sauce. We call this oil 'rogan' (derived from 'Roganjosh') and you can use it as a drizzle over other meals or as a basis for a dressing. Alternatively you can make your own rogan by slowly heating a spice or combination of spices with a neutral oil. This way you can build up a store of unique flavourings that give your creations a personal touch.

The recipes often call for tamarind pulp. This is easy to prepare: just soak the tamarind in warm water for some time, then pass it through a sieve.

Finally, I do recommend you prepare sauce bases (to freeze), spice mixes and masalas in larger quantities to cut down preparation time in subsequent meals. And don't forget that there are now a lot of good-quality pre-prepared ingredients on the supermarket shelves, such as peeled onions, ginger and garlic pastes, chutneys, pickles and so on, that are all great time-savers.

SEAFOOD

India has an extensive coastline, and naturally the coastal regions are where most of the country's wide variety of seafood dishes originate. In fact, there is such an abundance of seafood dishes in Indian cuisine that it was hard to limit myself to listing only a few recipes here.

The type of fish or seafood used in the following recipes is not necessarily the traditional choice—for example, a lot of dishes from the eastern states of India use carp, which is available only in that region. So here I have picked from what is available to me, in Sydney, that will suit the composition and the preparation of each dish.

You may replace the fish or seafood with what is locally available to you. Just remember that the fish you choose should be close in texture to what the recipe recommends, in order to deliver a similar result.

In the following recipes, I have used different types of seafood and different cooking methods to demonstrate how seafood can be prepared in various styles.

karwari jheenga

semolina crusted prawns

Hailing from a region called Karwar on the west coast, this makes an excellent starter for a meal
if you use small to medium-sized prawns.

SERVES: 4

3 tsp tamarind pulp

20 medium raw prawns

2 cloves garlic

salt

1 tsp chilli powder

½ tsp ground turmeric

2 cups coarse semolina

oil to shallow-fry

Prepare the tamarind pulp (see page 9). Peel, devein and wash the prawns thoroughly; drain and dry them well. Peel the garlic and crush to a fine paste. Sprinkle salt on the prawns, rub in well and set aside for a few minutes. In a bowl mix the chilli powder, turmeric, garlic and tamarind pulp. Marinate the prawns in this mixture for at least half an hour. Crumb them with semolina, pressing them firmly between the palms.

Heat oil in a pan. Shallow-fry the prawns on medium heat until golden brown. Turn them over to allow them to cook and colour evenly. Drain on a paper towel to remove excess oil, and serve hot.

Fresh coconut chutney (Nalikera chutney, see recipe page 180) is the traditional accompaniment for this dish. It can also be served with a salad. The prawns in this recipe may be replaced with large ones or scampi or any other fish that can be pan-fried.

chemmeen mapas

prawns in coconut milk

Immensely popular with the Christians of Kerala, a southern state, this is a flavoursome broth-like dish.
Very easy to prepare, it's a light dish for any season.

SERVES: 4

2 tbsp tamarind pulp

24 raw prawns

salt

½ tsp ground turmeric

6 golden shallots

4 cloves garlic

4 cm (1½ in.) piece ginger

4 green chillies

½ cup oil

½ tsp black mustard seeds

1 sprig fresh curry leaves

1 tbsp ground coriander

1 cup coconut cream

2 sprigs fresh coriander

Prepare tamarind pulp (see page 9). Peel, devein and wash prawns. Marinate with salt and half the turmeric. Slice shallots and garlic, and cut ginger into fine julienne. Deseed chillies and cut into strips.

Heat oil in a heavy-based pan. Add mustard seeds and curry leaves, and follow immediately with the sliced shallots and garlic. Sauté well, then add the ginger and chillies. Add the remaining turmeric and the ground coriander to this mix and then the prawns. Add the coconut cream and bring to a gentle boil, stirring occasionally. Add the tamarind pulp and salt to taste. Cook on a low heat for 5–7 minutes, until prawns are cooked.

Serve hot, garnished with sprigs of coriander.

The prawns may be substituted with other seafood, such as scallops or lobster. Traditionally, firm white fish is cooked in the same way as well. The heat level depends on the type and quantity of green chilli used.

Serve with steamed rice.

patra-ni-macchi

fish with green chutney in banana leaves

For this Parsi celebration dish, fish is traditionally steamed in banana leaves with green chutney.
Here, I have given a couple of alternatives for ease.

SERVES: 4

800 g (1 lb 12 oz) flathead fillets
salt
6 green chillies
1½ cups fresh coconut, grated
   or 1 cup desiccated coconut
½ bunch fresh coriander
1 tsp cumin seeds
8 cloves garlic
2 tsp sugar
2 tsp lemon juice
banana leaves or foil to wrap fish

Skin and clean fish and cut into strips. Season lightly with salt, set aside. Slit the chillies and remove the seeds (this dish is not intended to be very hot). Grind coconut, coriander, chillies, cumin, garlic, sugar and lemon juice into a paste. Coat each strip of fish with the paste. Wrap each fish strip in a piece of banana leaf and secure gently by tying if required. Use foil if banana leaves are not available. Remember to grease the foil lightly to prevent sticking.

Place in a steamer and steam until the fish is cooked. Alternatively, lay them in a baking tray and bake in a preheated 180°C (350°F/gas 4) oven until the fish is cooked.

I find that flathead fillets produce the best result, but this marinade can be tried on any freshwater flat fish fillets.

An ideal accompaniment is Rice and lentil mix Parsi style (Parsi kitchdi, see recipe page 147). The simplicity and the taste of this combination make it one of my favourites. Chilli oil may be used for garnish to give a hint of heat, without taking away the fragrance and sweetish finish.

rawas fry

pan-fried trout

Fried fish, curry and rice is the staple diet in Goa. The abundance of a variety of seafood available in this region makes dishes such as this daily fare for the locals.

SERVES: 4

1 tbsp tamarind pulp

4 x180 g (6½ oz) trout fillets (skin on)

2.5 cm (1 in.) piece ginger

6 cloves garlic

salt

¼ tsp ground turmeric

1 tsp chilli powder

rice flour to dust fish

oil to shallow-fry

Prepare tamarind pulp (see page 9). Clean fish and ensure there are no scales left on the skin. Score the skin gently to make slits. Peel ginger and garlic and grind to a fine paste. Apply salt and turmeric to the fish and set aside. Mix chilli powder with the ground ginger and garlic paste and tamarind pulp. Marinate the fish in this mix for about an hour.

Dust the fish with rice flour. Heat the oil in a pan and shallow-fry the fish on gentle heat on the skin side first to get a crispy finish. Turn over and cook the other side lightly to keep the fish moist.

This recipe may be used with any fish. Flat freshwater fish cutlets work well, because the centre bone keeps the fish moist and firm enough to handle the marinade and the cooking. Retaining the skin is a matter of personal preference. I have left the skin on for this recipe as it keeps the fish moist.

Combining this recipe with the Mussel curry (Xinaneanche kodi, see recipe page 19) and rice with some traditional Pickled prawn relish (Balchao, see recipe page 184) makes a standard Goan meal.

xinaneanche kodi

mussel curry

The sauce base in this recipe is very versatile and can be used to cook a variety of seafood, either individually or as a combination. This is a classic from Goa.

SERVES: 4

2 tbsp tamarind pulp

1 kg (2 lb 4 oz) mussels

6 cloves garlic

2 large onions

½ cup oil

1 tsp ground turmeric

4 green chillies

2½ cups fresh coconut, grated
  or 2 cups coconut cream

8 dried red chillies
  or 1 tbsp Kashmiri chilli powder

1½ tbsp coriander seeds

1 tbsp black peppercorns
  or 1 tsp freshly ground
  black pepper

salt

Prepare tamarind pulp (see page 9). Clean and beard the mussels. Peel garlic and crush into a paste. Chop a quarter of an onion finely. Heat a little oil in a heavy-based pan. Add chopped onion, a pinch of turmeric and ½ teaspoon of the crushed garlic. Sauté well and add the mussels. Pour in ½ cup of water, cover and steam for just a short while. When the shells open up, remove mussels and drain. Slice the remaining onions, slit green chillies and set aside.

   To prepare a spice paste for the sauce, either,

a) Combine grated coconut, red chillies (may be soaked in warm water for ease), coriander seeds, remaining turmeric, garlic and peppercorns in a blender and grind well with some water into a fine paste. Or,

b) Combine the powdered ingredients with coconut cream.

   Heat remaining oil in a pan. Add sliced onions and slit chillies and sauté lightly. Add the coconut mix. The results will be very different (texture and flavour) depending on which mix is used. Simmer for about 10 minutes on gentle heat. Do not boil vigorously. Add the tamarind pulp and stir. Add mussels and stir well for a couple of minutes. Taste for salt and remove from heat.

If you cook other seafood in the same sauce, vary the cooking times accordingly. If using the coconut cream and powdered ingredients, the preparation is very quick. Although it may not taste absolutely authentic, it does give a good result. When available, try replacing tamarind with raw green mango (peeled and sliced thinly).

Fish curry is traditionally served with rice. Try combining it with the Pan-fried trout (Rawas fry, see recipe page 18) and the Pickled prawn relish (Balchao, see recipe page 184).

surmai tawa masala

griddle-fried kingfish fillets

A typical dish from the western state of Maharashtra that is very simple and easy to prepare.

SERVES: 4

500 g (1 lb 2 oz) kingfish fillets
salt
juice of 1 lemon
½ tsp ground turmeric
1 tbsp chilli powder
1 tsp cumin seeds
1 tsp coriander seeds
½ tsp black peppercorns
3 shallots
1 cm (½ in.) piece ginger
4 cloves garlic
1 sprig fresh curry leaves
oil to pan-fry

Slice the fish fillets to desired size, sprinkle with some salt, lemon juice and turmeric and set aside for a few minutes. Put the rest of the ingredients except oil in a blender and puree until smooth. Smear the fish fillets with this paste and marinate for at least an hour. For convenience or ease of preparation, the coriander seeds, cumin seeds and black peppercorns may be replaced with ready-made powders of the same ingredients; however, the taste will be slightly different.

The fish should be cooked on a griddle ideally, but you can use a pan. The pan will need more oil than a griddle. Cook on a moderate heat until the spice mix gets darker and forms a firm coating on the fish. Turn the pieces over gently and cook in the same way on the other side.

This marinade can be used on other fish as well. Either a cutlet of a large white fish or whole fish can be used. If marinating whole fish, score the fish on both sides so the marinade can penetrate. When cooking over direct flame, it should be an even, gentle heat, as the spices could burn.

Serve with the traditional Maharashtrian salad (Koshumbir, see recipe page 100) and Garlic chutney (Lasanachi chutney, see recipe page 180). It could be eaten with a simple green salad with lemon dressing too.

shorshe bata maach

fish in mustard sauce

An extremely popular East Indian curry. I find this simple recipe sharp and
different to the regular notion of a 'fish curry'.

SERVES: 4

750 g (1 lb 10 oz) swordfish fillets
salt
1½ tsp ground turmeric
½ cup brown mustard seeds
3 cm (1¼ in.) piece ginger
8 green chillies
½ tsp ground cumin
½ tsp ground coriander
½ cup mustard oil (preferable)
    or vegetable oil
juice of ½ lemon

Clean the fish and cut into desired size. Sprinkle with some salt and
turmeric and set aside. Place mustard seeds, ginger, green chillies, cumin
and coriander in a blender and grind into a fine paste.

Heat half the oil in a pan. Place drained fish in very hot oil just to
seal both sides, then remove. Add the remaining oil and bring it back
to a high temperature. Add the ground paste, stir and cook well. Add
some water when required to prevent sticking or burning. Add fish to
the sauce and simmer gently until cooked. Finish off with lemon juice.
Taste and adjust the seasoning.

Hilsa, the fish that is traditionally used in this dish, is very bony. I have used
swordfish, but you could use any firm fish with strong flavour.

This dish is usually served with rice. I would also recommend Battered pumpkin
flowers (see recipe page 101), which is better known to the people of this
region as 'Kumro phool'.

chettinad meen varuval

south indian fried fish

A truly outstanding recipe from Chettinad. Very simple to prepare and yet extremely tasty.

SERVES: 4

4 x 150 g (5½ oz) mackerel steaks
½ tsp ground turmeric
salt
1 tsp ground cumin
1 tbsp ground coriander
1 tsp chilli powder
½ tsp fennel seeds
½ sprig fresh curry leaves
3 shallots
2 cloves garlic
juice of 1 lime
oil to pan-fry

Sprinkle fish with some turmeric and salt and set aside. In a small bowl mix the rest of the turmeric, cumin, coriander, chilli powder and crushed fennel seeds and set aside. Shred the curry leaves and peel shallots and garlic. Put curry leaves, shallots and garlic into a blender and grind into a paste. Add this paste with the lime juice and a little water (if required) to the spice mix and stir to form a thick paste. Smear the fish with this mix and marinate for an hour.

Heat oil in a pan and pan-fry the fish until almost crisp. Turn over and repeat on the other side to finish cooking.

Seer fish is traditionally used in this dish but is not available everywhere. Mackerel gives a similar result. The marinade is usually very spicy and salty, and some people use tamarind pulp instead of lime juice for sourness. Adjust all these three tastes to suit your palate. This dish cooks well on a grill too.

To cut through the spicy and tart flavours, I recommend another classic from Chettinad: Cucumber with split yellow lentils (Vellarikka kootu, see recipe page 104).

mahi aur simla mirch ka soola

tandoori fish fillets with capsicum

The traditional 'fish tikka' is cooked in the 'tandoor', the clay oven, so this is a slight variation. I have chosen wild barramundi as it lends itself well to the marinade and cooks well in the intense heat.

SERVES: 4

1 cup yoghurt
800 g (1 lb 12 oz) wild
    barramundi fillets
salt
juice of 2 lemons
2.5 cm (1 in.) piece ginger
6 cloves garlic
2 large capsicums
2 tbsp cream
½ tsp carom seeds
1 tbsp chilli powder
oil to baste (optional)

Put the yoghurt in a strainer lined with muslin cloth for about 2 hours to drain off all the whey. Select the centre cut of large fillets that are skinned and boned. Cut the fish into 5–6 cm (2–2½ in.) cubes. Sprinkle with some salt and lemon juice and set aside. Peel ginger and garlic and grind together into a fine paste in a blender with a little water. Cut the capsicums to the same size as the fish and place in a separate bowl with some salt and lemon juice. Place the yoghurt, cream, ground ginger and garlic, carom seeds and chilli powder in a bowl and blend with a whisk. Place the fish into this mix, adjust the seasoning and marinate for 3 hours.

Thread the fish and capsicum alternately onto skewers. Preheat the tandoor or charcoal grill. Cook for 6 minutes, remove and rest the skewers to let the excess moisture drain and collect in a tray. Just prior to serving, resume cooking for a further 3 minutes. Alternatively, this can be cooked in the oven. Preheat the oven to 200°C (400°F/gas 6). It will need a longer cooking time than on a grill. Baste with some oil.

You can use any fish that is thick-fleshed and slightly oily as an alternative to barramundi. Monitor the cooking time closely as the fish could dry out rapidly in the high heat.

My 'Tandoori' salad (see recipe page 127) can accompany most grilled items from the tandoor. This salad would make the best accompaniment for this dish, along with some Mint chutney (Pudhina chutney, see recipe page 178) and Layered bread (Laccha paratha, see recipe page 132).

methi suva macchi

tuna with fenugreek and dill leaves

We created this recipe for a special occasion we once held at the Taj in Bombay. We used a baby pomfret then, but when I tried it again with tuna the result was even better.

SERVES: 4

600 g (1 lb 5 oz) yellowfin tuna fillets
½ bunch fresh fenugreek
¼ bunch fresh dill
¼ bunch fresh spearmint
¼ bunch fresh coriander
2 green chillies
½ tsp fennel seeds
salt
oil to pan-fry
juice of 1 lemon

Trim tuna fillets and cut into thick steaks. Pick and chop all the herb leaves individually. Slit green chillies, remove all the seeds and chop finely. Dry-roast fennel seeds very lightly on a gentle heat, and crush with mortar and pestle. In a bowl mix the chopped herbs, chillies, fennel seeds and some salt.

Season the tuna with salt. Heat oil and quickly seal tuna in a very hot pan. Sprinkle with some lemon juice then roll in the chopped herb mix. Press between the palms of your hands to get all the greens to adhere to the tuna. Place on an oiled baking tray. Cook in a preheated 180°C (350°F/gas 4) oven to the desired degree of doneness, roughly 3 minutes.

If fresh fenugreek is not available, use dried fenugreek but reduce the quantity because the taste varies drastically. The seeds from the chillies are completely removed in this recipe as the desired result is not too spicy, but you can adjust the chilli to suit your palate.

The sweet and tart Tomato relish called 'Tamatar ka kut' (see recipe page 182) is an ideal accompaniment.

veloori varathathu

crispy fried whitebait

Veloori is a small white fish like a sardine that is popular in Kerala, the southern state where this recipe hails from. Whitebait gives a fairly close result.

SERVES: 4

1 tbsp tamarind pulp
650 g (1 lb 7 oz) large whitebait
2 cloves garlic
1 tbsp chilli powder
½ tsp ground turmeric
salt
1 cup rice flour
oil to deep-fry

Prepare the tamarind pulp (see page 9). Clean the fish well under running water until completely rid of the scales. Drain and dry well. Grind garlic, chilli and turmeric into a fine paste. Mix with the tamarind pulp and some salt. Marinate the fish in this mix and set aside for at least half an hour.

Dust the fish with rice flour. Deep-fry in hot oil until golden brown and crispy.

Try the same marinade with sardine fillets.

Serve with Fresh coconut chutney (Nalikera chutney, see recipe page 180). With a salad it is an ideal starter. On its own, it can make a good snack.

teesrya koshumbiri

warm clam salad

Interestingly there is a distinct difference between the styles of this dish practised by the Christians and Hindus in Goa. This recipe gives the Hindu, or Marathi, version.

SERVES: 4

2 kg (4 lb 8 oz) clams
salt
2 onions
3 tomatoes
3 green chillies
4 cloves garlic
½ cup oil
1 tsp cumin seeds
½ tsp ground turmeric
2 cups fresh coconut, grated
3 sprigs fresh coriander
1 tsp garam masala (optional)*

Wash clams well under running water to remove all the sand. Put them in a pot with some salt and water and boil for 3 minutes. Drain the water and separate the shells. Retain the shell with the flesh and discard the empty half. Chop onions, tomatoes, chillies and garlic.

Heat oil in a wok or sauté pan. Add cumin seeds and cook until they crackle. Add the onions, chillies and garlic. Sauté gently without colouring. Add turmeric and then the tomatoes. When the mix is sautéed well, add the clams and cook for a couple of minutes, stirring constantly. Add the coconut and mix well. Add salt if required. Finish off with coriander leaves. Sprinkle with some garam masala (optional).

*The recipe for Garam masala (Aromatic spice mix) can be found on page 190.

This recipe can also be made with mussels or prawns.

Because this is really a home-style recipe, I would present it simply with some boiled organic red rice. The combination is very earthy in its flavours. It works well with a green salad as well.

macchi amritsari

battered fish

Being a seafood dish, this recipe—from the northern region of Punjab—stands out because the state is not coastal.
This dish was made popular by the truckie pit stops along the road to Amritsar.
Traditionally pomfret or another firm white fish is used.

SERVES: 4

700 g (1 lb 9 oz) wild
    barramundi fillets
salt
juice of 2 lemons
¼ tsp ground turmeric
2 cm (³/₄ in.) piece ginger
6 cloves garlic
2 cups chickpea flour
½ tsp chilli powder
¼ tsp carom seeds
1 small egg
oil to deep-fry
½ tsp chaat masala

Clean the fish fillets and cut into long strips. Drain and dry on paper towel. Sprinkle with salt, half the lemon juice and the turmeric, and set aside. Peel ginger and garlic and grind into a paste. Prepare a batter with chickpea flour, ground ginger and garlic, chilli powder, carom seeds, beaten egg, salt and some water. The consistency of the batter has to be fairly thick.

Heat oil in a deep pan until moderately hot. Dip the fish strips in the batter to coat well. Deep-fry until golden brown. Sprinkle some chaat masala and lemon juice on the fish as soon as it is removed from the oil.

'Chaat' masala is a proprietary spice mix available in most Indian spice shops, composed of black salt, dried mango and other spices that add to the flavour of fish. It keeps well on the shelf and is worth having in the pantry for use with many North Indian recipes.

You could serve this just with some Mint chutney (Pudhina chutney, see recipe page 178), but I would also add some salad.

talshilele pedve

spicy sardines

A classic, yet uncommon, Mangalorean recipe. Seafood is daily fare for the people of this region, and sardines are one of the most popular fish. The Kanara region, where this recipe hails from, has a very rich culinary heritage.

SERVES: 4

1 tbsp tamarind pulp
800 g (1 lb 12 oz) sardine fillets
salt
½ tsp ground turmeric
2 tbsp oil
¼ tsp asafoetida
1 tsp ground coriander
½ tsp chilli powder

Prepare tamarind pulp (see page 9). Clean and dry the fish. Sprinkle with salt and turmeric, and set aside.

Heat a pan and add oil. Add the asafeotida and then the rest of the spice powders. Add tamarind pulp and salt, and stir well. Add ½ cup of water to help cooking. Simmer and reduce until almost all of the water has evaporated and the spices are cooked. Add more water and repeat the process. Then place the sardines in this mix and simmer. Turn them over and cook on the other side until the spices completely coat the fish.

This is a truly simple and very authentic recipe. The technique is unique—it is somewhere between sautéing and braising. Sardines in this part of India are generally just gutted, heads removed, cleaned and cooked with the bones. The flesh is scored to let the spices penetrate. While it is cumbersome to eat the fish with the bones left in, it is much tastier. Coconut oil, which is abundantly available in the region, is traditionally used to cook this dish.

I like to serve this with another traditional yet lesser-known dish called 'Daal pulao' (Rice with yellow lentils, see recipe page 151) which is also unique in its preparation.

bharleli chimbori

stuffed crab

This recipe is from the state of Maharashtra on the west coast.

SERVES: 4

4 medium blue swimmer crabs

2 medium onions

4 green chillies

1 cm (½ in.) piece ginger

4 cloves garlic

2 medium tomatoes

5 sprigs fresh coriander

2 eggs

¾ cup oil

½ tsp ground turmeric

1 tsp ground coriander

salt

juice of 1 lime

Plunge the crabs into boiling water, remove and cool. Separate the claws and body and remove all the meat from the shells. Retain the centre shell intact; clean, dry and set aside for presentation. Dice onions finely; deseed and chop chillies; peel ginger and garlic and dice very finely. Blanch and finely dice the tomatoes; pick and chop the coriander leaves. Hard boil the eggs, then chop the whites and yolks separately.

Heat oil in a pan and add the chopped onions. Sauté until they start to colour. Add the chillies, ginger and garlic. Cook well. Add the turmeric and ground coriander and sauté. Then add the tomatoes and a pinch of salt. Cook well. Add the crab meat and toss gently. Remove from the heat and sprinkle on lime juice and half the coriander leaves. Mix well. Divide the mix into 4 equal parts and fill the shells that were set aside. Top with chopped eggs and the remaining coriander leaves.

Although I have suggested the use of blue swimmer crabs here, this recipe will work well with large mud crabs too. However, the blue swimmer shells lend themselves to attractive presentation.

The filled crab shells is the traditional way of presenting this dish. You can also present it without the shells, and mould the crab mix instead. Serve with a salad and a lime and oil dressing. This not only presents well, but the tastes are delicate.

POULTRY

Chicken is the most popular meat for the non-vegetarians in India. Naturally there are hundreds of different dishes made with chicken, and here I have picked a blend of those that are popular, some that are less well known and some unique. I have suggested combinations of recipes that would complement each other to make the meal complete.

I must add a note here on the quality and flavour of poultry. In the modern world because of the problems associated with its production (hygiene regulations due to bird flu and pressures to cope with the demand to name a couple), the end product—which is the starting point for our recipes—loses a lot of flavour. So, pick poultry well to get better flavour. Use fresh birds from reputable farms that sell organic and free-range produce. Since we are using highly fragrant sauces or spice mixes, it is especially important to pick good-quality birds which will deliver the best experience. The same rule applies to all the other meats and vegetables too.

A lot of the authentic recipes use chicken with the bones left in. Here, I often use cuts of chicken where the bones are removed completely for convenience. However, cooking with the bones left in imparts more flavour and, depending on the occasion, it is worth a try. Bear in mind though that the cooking time will vary.

malmali kabab

'silky' grilled chicken

As the name suggests, this is a delicate dish. If handled well, it is very flavoursome
and has a melt-in-the-mouth effect.

SERVES: 4

16 chicken tenderloins
salt
juice of 1 lemon
½ cup raw cashews
4 cloves garlic
pinch saffron
½ cup cream
2 sprigs fresh spearmint
1½ cups yoghurt
1 tsp garam masala*
½ tsp ground white pepper
1 tbsp oil
clarified butter to baste

Trim the chicken, sprinkle with some salt and lemon juice and set aside.
Soak cashews in a little warm water and blend to a smooth paste. Add
peeled garlic and blend until smooth. Soak saffron in warmed cream
for a few minutes to release its flavour. Shred the mint leaves finely. In
a bowl, whisk together yoghurt, cashew and garlic paste, saffron cream,
garam masala, white pepper, oil and mint. Marinate the chicken in this
mix for at least 3 hours.

Thread the chicken onto metal skewers and cook in a tandoor oven
or over a charcoal grill if possible. Alternatively, cook skewers on a rack in
a preheated 190°C (375°F/gas 5) oven for 7 minutes. Being delicate, these
fillets cook very rapidly. Baste with clarified butter during cooking.

*The recipe for Garam masala (Aromatic spice mix) can be found on page 190.

An excellent starter, this also makes a good choice for those who cannot eat
chillies.

As for most other tandoori kebabs, the ideal accompaniments are the Mint
chutney (Pudhina chutney, see recipe page 178), salad and bread.

galinha cafreal

goan grilled chicken

A Goan classic, this is very popular among the locals. Although most Goan cooks fry the chicken for this dish,
I have taken a healthier option.

SERVES: 4

1 whole 600 g (1 lb 5 oz) spring
   chicken or spatchcock
salt
juice of 2 lemons
2 cm (³/₄ in.) piece ginger
5 green chillies
4 cloves garlic
½ bunch fresh coriander
1 tbsp coriander seeds
1 tbsp cumin seeds
1 tbsp black peppercorns
1½ tbsp oil

Prepare the chicken for grilling by removing the backbone and laying the bird flat. Sprinkle with some salt and the lemon juice and set aside for half an hour. Grind ginger, chillies, garlic and fresh coriander (with the stalk and roots) into a fine paste. Dry-grind coriander seeds, cumin seeds and peppercorns into a fine powder and add it to the green paste. Mix well and marinate the chicken in this mix for 4 hours in the fridge.

Brush oil on a grill and seal the chicken. Transfer to a baking tray and cover with foil to prevent burning and to keep the chicken moist. Finish cooking in a preheated 180°C (350°F/gas 4) oven for 30 minutes. Remove the chicken from the tray and cut up into legs and breasts. Deglaze the pan with ¹/₂ cup water to make some juice to serve with the chicken.

This makes an excellent barbecue item. I have experimented with this marinade on duck and it works really well.

Serve with some crusty bread or roast potatoes. I also like it with Mince-filled potato patties (Goan potato chops, see recipe page 102) and some salad. Truly a very 'bistro-ish' act—very earthy fare.

koli melagu varuval

pepper chicken chettinad

There are several versions of this classic dish from the south of India. When I visited the south and actually saw this being prepared by an expert from this region I was surprised to see the simplicity of the dish.

SERVES: 4

4 chicken breast fillets
salt
½ tsp ground turmeric
8 shallots
12 cloves garlic
1 tsp fennel seeds
6 dried red chillies
1 tbsp black peppercorns
5 tomatoes
½ cup oil

Clean and trim the chicken breasts. (I prefer the skin left on because it keeps the meat moist.) Sprinkle with salt and turmeric and set aside. Peel the shallots and garlic. Dry-roast half the fennel seeds with chillies and peppercorns on gentle heat, stirring constantly. Crush using a pestle and mortar. Crush the shallots and garlic in a blender, then mix in the pounded spices. Chop up the tomatoes roughly.

Heat oil in a heavy-based pan. Put in the rest of the fennel seeds and then the chicken breasts. Seal well on all sides and remove. Add the tomatoes and some salt. Stir and cook well. Add the garlic, shallot and spice mix. Cook on a moderate heat, stirring constantly. Return the chicken to the pan and simmer until fully cooked.

Traditionally, fenugreek seeds are added with the fennel seeds right at the beginning. It is important to watch the fenugreek very closely while cooking, as it turns bitter if overcooked. I have used chicken breasts in this recipe but this dish can be prepared with chicken drumsticks or thigh fillets too.

I serve the classical vegetable dish Stir-fried green beans (Beans porial, see recipe page 110) with this chicken. Fried potatoes 'like fish' (Kizhangu karuvadu varuval, see recipe page 105) from this region works well too. Accompany with Lemon rice (Elumikkai sadam, see recipe page 148).

tulsi ke tikke

chicken with basil

At Qmin, this is one of the signature dishes and it has been on the menu since the opening of the restaurant.

SERVES: 4

500 g (1 lb 2 oz) chicken thigh fillets
2 cm (³/₄ in.) piece ginger
5 cloves garlic
1 bunch fresh Vietnamese basil
1 green chilli
¼ cup raw cashews
½ cup oil
1 tsp garam masala*
1 tsp chaat masala
salt

Clean the chicken thigh meat and cut into cubes. Peel ginger and garlic. Pick the basil leaves and chop the chilli. Soak the cashews in warm water for 30 minutes. Puree the ginger and garlic in the blender, then add the basil, cashews and chillies with half the oil and blend well into a fine paste. Remove from the blender, add garam masala, chaat masala and salt. Mix the chicken well with the prepared marinade and add the rest of the oil. Marinate for at least 4 hours.

Thread the chicken onto skewers and cook on a charcoal grill (for better flavour) or on a barbecue or, alternatively, in a preheated 180°C (350°F/gas 4) oven or grill.

*The recipe for Garam masala (Aromatic spice mix) can be found on page 190.

At Qmin this is cooked on metal skewers in a 'tandoor', the Indian clay oven.

This really versatile marinade works well with other meats, seafood or even vegetables. We have used it on salmon, trout, eggplant and quail. It is best prepared fresh when ready to use. The finished dish in this recipe is mild, but the heat depends on the type and number of green chillies used. Chaat masala can be bought prepared from any Indian spice store. Garam masala may also be purchased, but made fresh, the result is very different.

Serve with any traditional bread and some salad.

farcha

fried chicken parsi style

Here is an unusual recipe for chicken, as popularly made by the Parsi community in Bombay.

SERVES: 4

4 chicken breast fillets
1 medium onion
2 cm (³/₄ in.) piece ginger
4 cloves garlic
1 tsp cumin seeds
½ bunch fresh coriander
salt
1 tbsp plain flour
1 tbsp oil
breadcrumbs to coat
2 eggs
oil to deep-fry

Score each chicken breast to allow the marinade to penetrate. Put roughly chopped onion, ginger, garlic, cumin and coriander into a blender and puree to a fine paste. Transfer to a bowl and add a pinch of salt, flour and oil. Coat each chicken breast with the marinade and rest for at least 3 hours. When marinating is complete, roll the chicken breasts in breadcrumbs. Beat the eggs until light.

Heat oil in a deep pan for frying. Dip each chicken breast in beaten egg and fry until golden brown. Drain to remove excess oil.

If using large pieces of chicken or leg pieces, par-boil the meat before crumbing it.

Parsi tomato sauce (see recipe page 185) usually accompanies this dish.

pista badam murg

chicken with pistachios and almonds

Very fragrant and mild, this classical recipe from Hyderabad is usually a special occasion dish, as it takes more time to prepare than most other recipes in this book.

SERVES: 4

2 whole 700 g (1 lb 9 oz)
    spring chickens
salt
4 onions
2 cm (^{3}/$_4$ in.) piece ginger
4 cloves garlic
1 cup ghee
6 green chillies
6 cardamom pods
½ cup peeled almonds
½ cup peeled pistachios
½ cup cream
pinch saffron
1½ cups yoghurt
1 tsp black peppercorns
2 bay leaves
6 cloves

Separate the legs and breasts from the chickens. Split each chicken in half as for grilling, discarding the backbone. Clean well, wash and drain. Sprinkle with salt and set aside. Peel onions. Cut half the onions into chunks and boil with some water, then puree. Slice the remaining onions very finely, sprinkle with a pinch of salt and set aside for a few minutes. Peel ginger and garlic, place in a blender and grind together into a paste, adding some water if required. Squeeze out the sliced onions in muslin cloth to remove all the juice. Heat ghee in a pan and fry the onions until golden brown, stirring to attain even colour. Drain onions and set aside, saving the ghee for use later. When onions are cool, puree into a paste. Slit green chillies. Dry-roast half the cardamom, then pound well. Chop up almonds and pistachios, slicing some for garnish. Warm a little cream and soak saffron in it. In a bowl, combine the boiled onion puree, ginger and garlic paste, yoghurt and some salt, and whisk to obtain an even consistency.

Place the chicken on a roasting pan, skin-side facing up. Sprinkle with peppercorns, bay leaves, cloves and chillies, and pour the onion mix over. Seal tightly with a lid or foil. Bake in a preheated 180°C (350°F/gas 4) oven for about 35 minutes. Remove chicken from pan. Strain the sauce from the pan, then add it to the pan that contains the reserved ghee. Put the pan back on medium heat. Add the chopped nuts, saffron cream and the browned onion paste. Bring to the boil, stirring gently. Finish off with remaining cream and ground cardamom. Check for seasoning and pour over the chicken. Garnish with sliced almonds and pistachios.

Traditionally the chicken is smoked using a process called 'dungaar'. When the chicken is just out of the oven, place a small metal bowl with a whole cardamom pod in it in the centre of the pan. Place a small piece of burning coal in it and spoon over a teaspoon of ghee. Cover the tray quickly and leave it for a few minutes. Remove the bowl and discard the contents. Although optional, this process adds a fantastic smoked aroma to the preparation.

The chicken is usually decorated with beaten silver leaf and nuts.

tharavu moilee

duck in coconut sauce

Duck is popular among certain parts of the meat-eating population. This dish is well known among the Christian community of the southern state of Kerala.

SERVES: 4

1 whole 1.8 kg (4 lb) free-range duck
salt
½ tsp ground turmeric
1 tbsp white vinegar
2 tbsp tamarind pulp
4 medium red onions
3 cm (1 ¼ in.) piece ginger
6 cloves garlic
6 green chillies
3 cardamom pods
1 tbsp black peppercorns
1 tsp ground coriander
2½ cups coconut milk
½ cup oil
1 tsp black mustard seeds
4 shallots
1 sprig fresh curry leaves

Joint the duck and separate the breasts and legs. Cut up the rest of the bones into large chunks and place in a roasting pan. Marinate the duck breasts and legs with some salt, turmeric and vinegar; set aside for at least an hour. Prepare the tamarind pulp (see page 9). Slice the onions, cut the ginger and garlic into strips and slit the green chillies. Sprinkle the onions, ginger, garlic and chillies over the duck bones and add cardamom, peppercorns, ground coriander and tamarind pulp. Pour on the coconut milk and add some salt. Blend the ingredients with a ladle. Place the duck legs and breasts on top.

Place the tray in a preheated 160°C (315°F/gas 2–3) oven and braise for at least 2 hours. The flesh should be soft and falling off the bone easily. Remove the duck pieces carefully and place them on a serving tray, or portion as desired. Strain the liquid from the tray into a pan and skim off all the fat. Reduce the sauce further until you get a gravy-like consistency, and pour over the duck. Heat oil in a small pan. Add mustard seeds and finely chopped shallots, followed by the curry leaves. Pour over the duck. (This method of finishing sauces is called tempering.) Gently shake the pan or container for the tempering to evenly spread.

This may be prepared in a pot instead of braising. The result would be slightly different.

The duck meat could be separated from the bone for serving, however the meat is very soft and falls off the bones easily.

east indian pot roast

pot roast of whole chicken

A unique recipe, classical to a community referred to as 'East Indians'. I was fortunate enough to have worked with a chef who shared with me this very special recipe he procured from his mother.

SERVES: 4

1 whole 1 kg (2 lb 4 oz) spring chicken
   or 2 whole 600 g (1 lb 5 oz)
   spatchcock

salt

10 dried red chillies

2 cm (³/₄ in.) piece ginger

5 cloves garlic

1 tbsp cumin seeds

3 cardamom pods

1 cinnamon stick

1 tsp black peppercorns

4 cloves

1½ cups brown vinegar

1 tsp sugar

1½ cups oil

500 g (1 lb 2 oz) button mushrooms

15 brown shallots

8 baby carrots

8 new potatoes

Clean and drain the chicken. Rub salt all over and set aside. Break the chillies into small pieces and discard the seeds. Peel ginger and garlic. Mix the chillies, ginger, garlic and all the dry whole spices and soak in vinegar for 2 hours. Blend the mix into a fine paste in a food processor. Add sugar and half the oil, mix well and rub onto the chicken. Peel and trim all the vegetable accompaniments, then sprinkle with some salt.

Heat a heavy-based roasting pot. Pour in the rest of the oil and seal the chicken on all sides. Lay the chicken on its back. Place the shallots around it. Add ½ cup of water to prevent the spices from burning, and place in a preheated 180°C (350°F/gas 4) oven. Baste occasionally. When completely cooked (about half an hour), remove the chicken. Stand the pan juices for a few minutes to let the oil float to the surface. Skim carefully and return the oil to the pot. Add the vegetables and roast for 10 minutes, stirring occasionally to prevent sticking and to cook evenly.

Carve or separate the chicken joints and serve with the roasted vegetables and pan juices.

I have tried this recipe with duck and other fowl and it works just as well. The pan juices may be reduced and used as a sauce. This makes a really hearty 'share meal' for the table.

Usually served with some salad and bread rolls.

dum ka murg

chicken cooked sealed

'Dum', or cooking in a sealed pot, helps retain all the juices and fragrance. It also keeps the meat moist and is a style that was popular with the cooks of Nizams, ancient rulers of Hyderabad.

SERVES: 4

1 whole 1 kg (2 lb 4 oz) chicken
salt
juice of 1 lime
2 onions
1 cup ghee
1 tsp cardamom pods
1 tsp cumin seeds
2 cm (³/₄ in.) piece ginger
4 cloves garlic
5 green chillies
2 sprigs fresh coriander
2½ cups yoghurt
1 tsp chilli powder
pinch saffron

Joint the chicken into 4 pieces: 2 breasts and 2 legs. Sprinkle with some salt and the lime juice and set aside. Slice the onions finely and fry in the ghee until golden brown. Reserve ghee. Drain onions and crush when cool. Dry-roast cardamom and cumin separately over a gentle heat, then crush. Peel ginger and garlic and puree together with green chillies and coriander. Mix yoghurt with all the other ingredients, including the ghee used to fry the onions, in a bowl. Put the chicken into this mix and let it marinate for at least 2 hours.

Transfer the chicken and marinade to a casserole dish or similar thick pan with a tight-fitting lid. Put on high heat and bring to the boil. Reduce the heat to low, put on the lid and simmer for at least half an hour. Remove when the chicken is cooked.

Chicken fillets may be used instead. However, cooking it on the bone adds flavour to the sauce.

Because this dish is highly fragrant yet mild in terms of heat, I recommend serving it with some steamed basmati rice and Braised chillies (Mirchi ka salan, see recipe page 120), from the same region.

awadhi khuroos

chicken in the style of awadh

Lucknow used to be known as 'Awadh' and is renowned for its cuisine. Some of the recipes from this 'old cuisine' were way ahead of their time and truly stunning. The style of cooking was called 'dum pukht', meaning sealed and cooked.

SERVES: 4

4 x 125 g (4½ oz) chicken
    breast fillets
120 g (4¼ oz) paneer*
salt
½ tsp black cumin seeds
3 sprigs fresh spearmint
4 onions
1 cup ghee
¾ cup yoghurt
2 cardamom pods
½ tsp whole mace
pinch saffron
1 cup cream
6 tomatoes
3 cm (1¼ in.) piece ginger
8 cloves garlic
½ tsp ground turmeric
2 tsp chilli powder
2 tbsp slivered almonds

Trim the tenderloins off the chicken fillets. Slit the fillets down the middle, open out and flatten gently with a meat mallet. Chop up the tenderloins into tiny cubes for preparing a stuffing. Place cubed chicken in a bowl and mix with crumbled paneer, some salt, half of the cumin seeds and chopped mint. Divide filling into four and spread evenly on the chicken fillets. Roll up the fillets tightly and set aside. Slice two-thirds of the onions finely, sprinkle with some salt and squeeze in a muslin cloth to remove moisture. Heat ghee in a pan and fry onions to a golden brown colour, then spread out on paper towels. Retain the ghee for further cooking. Save some browned onions for garnish and puree the rest with the yoghurt until smooth. Gently dry-roast cardamom and mace, then grind to a powder. Soak saffron in warmed cream. Chop tomatoes.

Heat the reserved ghee in a deep pan. Add remaining cumin seeds and cook until they crackle. Chop the remaining onions finely and add to the pan. Sauté lightly then add chopped ginger and garlic, and stir well. Add turmeric, chilli powder and tomatoes. Cook well and add 3 cups of water. Bring to the boil and simmer well, stirring occasionally. Skim the oil that comes to the surface. When the sauce is well reduced, add the chicken rolls and seal pan with foil or a tight-fitting lid. Simmer until the chicken is just cooked. Lift the rolls of chicken out and place on a serving dish. Strain the stock through a fine sieve and return to the pan. Bring back to the boil, whisk in the onion and yoghurt paste and saffron cream. Finish off with cardamom and mace powder. Adjust the consistency by reducing the sauce, and season. Garnish with reserved browned onions, almonds and mint.

*'Paneer' is a home-made curd cheese (see recipe page 190). You may replace it with unflavoured fetta or fresh crumbly cheese.

I serve this dish with Eggplant Lucknow style (Lucknowi baingan, see recipe page 107) from the same region.

bathak peri-peri

roast duck with peri-peri

The key to this Goan recipe is the spicy peri-peri spice mix (or masala). It is very versatile and can be used not only with duck, but with chicken or other meat too.

SERVES: 4

15 dried red chillies

1½ cups malt vinegar

2 tbsp tamarind pulp

1 whole 1.8 kg (4 lb) free-range duck

2 onions

2 carrots

3 cm (1¼ in.) piece ginger

8 cloves garlic

1 tbsp cumin seeds

1 cinnamon stick

5 cloves

1 tsp black peppercorns

½ tsp cardamom seeds

salt

Cut up the chillies, discard the seeds and soak in vinegar for at least 2 hours. Prepare tamarind pulp (see page 9). Separate the legs and breasts of the duck. Cut up the neck and all the bones and trimmings into chunks and place in a roasting tray. Peel onions and carrots and chop into big chunks, then mix with the duck trimmings. Peel and chop up ginger and garlic. Dry-roast the whole spices in a pan over a low heat. Combine chillies, vinegar, tamarind, ginger, garlic and all the dry spices and grind into a fine paste, without the addition of any water. Rub the spice mix and salt on the duck and set aside for 1 hour.

Preheat the oven to 200°C (400°F/gas 6). Place the duck legs and breasts on the trimmings and vegetables. Roast in the oven, basting occasionally. Reduce the heat to 180°C (350°F/gas 4) once the duck starts to brown. Continue to baste. Roast until the duck is soft and fully cooked, approximately 1 hour. Once cooked, gently lift off the duck pieces and strain the juices into a bowl. Skim off the fat, then transfer the sauce to a saucepan. Simmer, skim and reduce the juices. Pour over the duck.

The duck trimmings and vegetables not only add flavour, but also prevent the duck from sticking to the roasting tray. Grinding chillies with the ingredients could take considerable time in regular grinders; you can use fine-quality chilli powder instead to save time. If stored carefully topped with some oil, this peri-peri spice mix can be stored for a long time in the refrigerator for use later.

In some households, vegetables such as cabbage and potatoes are cooked along with the duck in its spices and fat, which render their flavour to the accompanying vegetables. I prefer to cook the vegetables separately for a much more presentable result, while using the pan juices on the duck. See recipe page 121 for Cabbage with potatoes (Repolho e batata).

ishtoo

chicken stew

'Ishtoo' is the South Indian colloquial term for stew. A home-style recipe from the southern state of Kerala, this mild chicken dish with a base of fresh coconut extract is extremely popular. Some even have it for breakfast!

SERVES: 4

600 g (1 lb 5 oz) chicken thigh fillets
3 medium desiree potatoes
2 red onions
6 green chillies
3 cm (1¼ in.) piece ginger
¾ cup oil
5 cardamom pods
3 cloves
1 tsp black peppercorns
1 sprig fresh curry leaves
2½ cups coconut milk
salt
1 tbsp white vinegar

Dice the chicken fillets into 5 cm (2 in.) cubes. Peel the potatoes and dice slightly smaller than the chicken. Peel onions and cut into strips. Slit the chillies. Peel ginger and cut into thin strips.

Heat oil in a pan. Add cardamom, cloves, peppercorns and then the curry leaves. Add onion and sauté without colouring. Add ginger and chillies. Add chicken pieces and seal. Add the coconut milk and salt. If necessary, add some water to obtain a thin stew-like consistency. Add potatoes and simmer. Adjust the seasoning, add vinegar and remove from the heat when the chicken and potatoes are cooked, in about 10–12 minutes.

Traditionally the base is prepared with fresh coconut extract. Since this recipe uses coconut milk instead, choose a light one. If a thick cream is the only one available, adjust the consistency with a neutral chicken stock or some water.

Serve with a bread called 'Pathiri' (Rice flour flat bread, see recipe page 140). This combination is truly sensational.

do kism ke murg ki seekh

tandoori chicken two ways

Tandoori chicken is one of the most popular Indian chicken dishes and is often referred to as 'King of Kababs' in India itself. Chicken tikka has been made more popular in the Western world because it is morsels without the bones left in. Here's chicken tikka prepared with two different marinades.

SERVES: 4

800 g (1 lb 12 oz) chicken
    thigh fillets
salt
juice of 2 lemons
3 cm (1¼ in.) piece ginger
6 cloves garlic
5 green chillies
2 cups yoghurt
½ tsp ground cumin
1 tsp garam masala*
1 cup oil
1 tbsp mild red chilli powder
clarified butter to baste

Cut up the chicken into morsels. Marinate in some salt and the lemon juice, and set aside. In a blender, grind ginger and garlic together into a fine paste. Separately, deseed the chillies and grind into a paste. To prepare the marinades, divide all the ingredients except the chilli paste, chilli powder and clarified butter equally into 2 bowls, and mix each well. Put the red chilli powder in one of the bowls and the green chilli paste in the other. Divide the chicken into halves and marinate one half in each of these marinades for at least 3 hours.

Ideally, the chicken is threaded onto metal skewers and cooked in the tandoor. The skewers may also be cooked on a charcoal grill for a similar taste. Alternatively, they can be cooked in a preheated 200°C (400°F/gas 6) oven for 10 minutes. Ensure the chickens skewers are resting on a tray or rack and not touching the bottom or sides of the oven. In all the options above, remember to baste with clarified butter.

*The recipe for Garam masala (Aromatic spice mix) can be found on page 190.

Originally the bright red colour of chicken tikka was obtained by using a paste made from dried Kashmiri chillies. But most chefs use an artificial food colouring (some excessively, I may add) to give the chicken a bright red colour. I prefer to avoid the use of this artificial colour and hence have suggested the use of mild (yet bright red) chilli powder. The green chillies that we use are larger than regular chillies (almost the length of French green beans). Being mild even before deseeding, you can use larger quantities without making the dish very hot. Optionally, add a sprig each of mint and coriander leaves while pureeing the chillies.

This is ideally accompanied by my 'Tandoori' salad (see recipe page 127) and Crispy bread (Khasta roti, see recipe page 131). Serve some Mint chutney (Pudhina chutney, see recipe page 178) and the famous Butter sauce (Makhni, see recipe page 185) alongside.

coorgi chicken

fried chicken from coorg

Coorg is a town in the southern state of Karnataka. I have read a couple of different versions of where this dish came from, but whatever the origin, it is very popular with the ales in bars across the southern states.

SERVES: 4

750 g (1 lb 10 oz) chicken
 thigh fillets
2 onions
2.5 cm (1 in.) piece ginger
1 tsp cumin seeds
1 tbsp coriander seeds
1 tbsp black peppercorns
2.5 cm (1 in.) piece cinnamon stick
2 cloves garlic
1½ tbsp chilli powder
salt
½ cup oil
juice of ½ lemon

Clean chicken and cut into strips 1 cm ($^1/_2$ in.) wide. Peel and finely dice onions. Peel ginger and chop finely. Dry-roast cumin seeds, coriander seeds, peppercorns and cinnamon, and grind to a powder. Peel garlic and puree. Mix all the spices with garlic and some salt and marinate the chicken strips in this mix for 2 hours.

Heat oil in a pan, add ginger, then onions, and sauté well, stirring constantly until lightly coloured. Add chicken, continue to stir-fry. Sprinkle with some water if necessary to prevent the spices from burning. There should be no liquid left when the chicken is fully cooked. Finish off with lemon juice and remove from heat.

The chicken may be roasted with the spice mix or barbecued. Whichever you choose, it is best to cut up the chicken into strips as this dish is supposed to be a snack.

The chicken can be wrapped in Millet flour bread (Ragi roti, see recipe page 139), made in the same region. This dish is quite spicy. To offset and complement it, serve with Eggplant chutney (Brinjal gojju, see recipe page 178).

kombdichi sukhe

chicken cooked with 'dry' spice

As with many other Indian dishes the success lies in the preparation of the spice mix. This spicy stir-fry style dish comes from a special faction of the state of Maharashtra on the west coast.

SERVES: 4

2 tbsp tamarind pulp

600 g (1 lb 5 oz) chicken
    thigh fillets

1 tbsp white poppy seeds

2½ cups fresh coconut, grated

1 tsp cumin seeds

1 tbsp coriander seeds

1 tsp black peppercorns

1 tsp fennel seeds

5 cloves garlic

1 tbsp chilli powder

2 onions

½ cup oil

1 sprig fresh curry leaves

Prepare tamarind pulp (see page 9). Cut chicken into 1 cm (¹/₂ in.) cubes. Soak the poppy seeds in hot water for at least 2 hours. Roast the coconut gently in a pan until lightly browned. Separately dry-roast the cumin, coriander, peppercorns and fennel. Cool and grind to a powder. Peel garlic and combine with tamarind, drained poppy seeds and coconut. Grind into a coarse paste, without any water added. Add the powdered spices and chilli powder to this mix. Dice onions very finely.

Heat oil in a pan. Add curry leaves and let them splutter, then add the onions. Add chicken and sauté well. Add the spice mix and cook, stirring continuously. It is important to maintain the high heat, and keep stir-frying to avoid burning the mix.

Use desiccated coconut if fresh is not available. The chicken may be cut into large cubes; however, it is more difficult to keep the whole dish 'dry', as the chicken pieces release their juices.

I use a very special bread to layer this dish with called 'Bhakri' (Sorghum flour bread, see recipe page 138), which is authentic to this region. You could also add some Garlic chutney (Lasanachi chutney, see recipe page 180). It is true peasant-style food, and is very hearty.

LAMB

Traditionally, red meats are eaten more in the northern part of India because of the colder weather. Among the non-vegetarians, lamb is the most popular red meat. Actually, it is more often goat than lamb that is used as it is more readily available in India. In Australia, of course, it is the opposite, so I have written all these recipes using lamb. Just remember that you will generally have to increase the cooking times if you do choose to use goat meat.

In these recipes, I'm using really good-quality Australian lamb, which not only cooks fast, its flavours are better enjoyed when it is not overcooked. So although it is not common practice in Indian cuisine to leave the meat underdone (or even pink), I have taken that liberty in some of the recipes here to expose that possibility. This should only be done with top-quality, flavoursome meat.

nalli roganjosh

kashmiri lamb shanks

Roganjosh has rightly earned a reputation the world over as the 'King of Curries'. There are several versions. Even in Kashmir itself, where it hails from, it is prepared differently by different religious sects—each claiming authenticity. The following version with shanks is really hearty fare.

SERVES: 4

4 lamb shanks

4 red onions

2 cm (³/₄ in.) piece ginger

6 cloves garlic

5 tomatoes

½ tsp ground coriander

1½ tbsp paprika

1 tsp chilli powder

pinch saffron

1 cup oil

1 cinnamon stick

5 cloves

3 black cardamom pods

2 bay leaves

salt

½ tsp ground mace

2 sprigs fresh coriander

Clean the shanks. Slice onions finely. Peel ginger and garlic and grind into a fine paste. Cut up the tomatoes and puree in a blender. Mix the ginger and garlic paste and the ground coriander, paprika and chilli powder in a bowl with 2 tablespoons of water to form a paste. Soak saffron in some warm water.

Heat oil in a heavy-based pan. Add the cinnamon, cloves, cardamom and bay leaves. Add sliced onions. Sauté, stirring well, until golden brown. Remove one-third of the mixture, drain and save for garnish. Add the spice paste to the onion mix and cook, stirring well. Add the shanks and turn to seal. Cover and cook until the oil starts to separate. Add some salt and about 4 cups of water (enough to cover the meat) and bring to the boil on a high heat. Add the tomato puree. Once boiled, reduce the heat and simmer for at least half an hour. Finish off with the mace and saffron, and garnish with coriander sprigs.

Other cuts of meat could be tried in this sauce as well. Diced leg of lamb is used in the classical roganjosh. I have tried this with 'barra' (lamb leg chops) or an osso buco style cut of lamb or goat leg.

At Qmin we introduced this served with Crushed potatoes (Aloo ka bhurta, see recipe page 113) and it was well received. It could also be accompanied by Saffron pilaf (Zaffrani pulao, see recipe page 154) and some vegetables.

kamargah

twice-cooked lamb cutlets

One of the best-known lamb dishes from India comes from Kashmir and is called 'roganjosh'. Kamargah is a lesser known Kashmiri lamb dish, probably because it is not a 'curry'. This dish of battered lamb cutlets is delicately flavoured and a personal favourite. It is a part of the several dishes that together make a Kashmiri feast for a celebration, known as 'Wazawan'.

SERVES: 4

16 lamb cutlets
salt
4 cups milk
2 tsp fennel seeds
1 tsp ground mace
pinch saffron
1 cup yoghurt
1 tsp ground cloves
1 tbsp chilli powder
¼ cup ghee
½ cup chickpea flour
1 cup plain flour
   or chickpea flour to dust
oil to deep-fry

Trim the lamb cutlets and scrape the bones. Season with salt. Boil 3 cups of the milk with ½ cup of water, fennel seeds, mace and saffron. Place the lamb cutlets in this liquid and quickly return to the boil. Simmer for 3 minutes then remove from heat. Drain and rest the meat. Prepare a marinade by blending yoghurt, cloves, chilli powder, ghee and some salt. Marinate the cutlets when cool and set aside. Mix chickpea flour, the rest of the milk and a pinch of salt in a bowl and whisk well to prepare a batter.

Heat oil in a deep pan. Dust the cutlets in some plain flour or chickpea flour. Dip in the batter and deep-fry until golden brown.

Gauge the length of cooking by the weight of the cutlets, to ensure that the meat is not overcooked and remains juicy.

I like to serve this with a classic vegetable dish from the region called 'Hak' (Stir-fried kale, see recipe page 112).

kheema

minced lamb

Although mince is cooked everywhere in India, this is a North Indian version. I picked this recipe up while training at the Taj Mahal Hotel in Delhi several years ago. I still remember this as being one of the best kheema I have had.

SERVES: 4

3 onions

8 green chillies

2 cm (³/₄ in.) piece ginger

5 cloves garlic

2 cups yoghurt

½ tsp ground cinnamon

½ cup ghee

2 tsp cumin seeds

2 tsp chilli powder

1 kg (2 lb 4 oz) lamb mince

salt

½ cup fresh coriander

1 tsp garam masala*

Chop onions finely. Slit the green chillies and remove all the seeds. Peel ginger and garlic. In a blender, puree the ginger, garlic and green chillies. Beat the yoghurt in a bowl with cinnamon.

Heat ghee in a heavy-based pan. Add cumin seeds and cook until they crackle. Follow with onions. Sauté over moderate heat until golden brown, stirring all the time. Add the garlic mix and continue to cook. Add the chilli powder and cook until dry, or when the liquid has cooked out and the oil starts to separate. Add the mince and some salt. Stir on higher heat. When the mix is boiling, reduce heat and cook, stirring occasionally. Add the yoghurt and mix well. Simmer until the oil starts to separate and it gets a good consistency. Adjust seasoning. Finish off with chopped coriander and garam masala.

*The recipe for Garam masala (Aromatic spice mix) can be found on page 190.

If possible, make the mince yourself from lean leg of lamb, which has been cleaned of all the fat and sinews and minced fresh, just prior to use. You may purchase prepared mince off the shelf, but opt for lean meat. The flavour and cooking times will vary depending on the type of mince used—i.e. lamb or goat or beef.

I serve this with a unique bread from this region called 'Khasta roti' (Crispy bread, see recipe page 131) and Wok-fried baby corn and mushrooms (Makkai khumb kadhai, see recipe page 114).

irachi ularthiathu

pan-roasted lamb

A celebration dish among a specific Christian community from Kerala, this recipe is usually done like a roast with a whole lamb leg. I have just used the rump and accordingly adjusted the cooking style. It is a spicy dish for the winter months.

SERVES: 4

4 small lamb rumps
4 brown shallots
2 cm (³/₄ in.) piece ginger
4 cloves garlic
1 sprig fresh curry leaves
salt
½ tsp ground turmeric
2 tsp black peppercorns
2 tsp fennel seeds
2 tsp coriander seeds
6 dried red chillies
1 cup fresh coconut, grated
½ cup oil

Trim the lamb and prick with a skewer to allow the marinade to penetrate. Peel shallots, ginger and garlic. Blend these into a paste with curry leaves. Add salt and turmeric to the paste. Rub over the lamb and set aside. Dry-roast the peppercorns, fennel seeds, coriander seeds and chillies individually and crush them with a mortar and pestle. Dry-roast coconut on low heat until golden brown, stirring all the time (it burns very rapidly). Add to the crushed spice mix. Roll the lamb in this mix and press down well so that the mix sticks to the lamb.

Heat oil in a roasting pan. Seal the meat on all sides quickly, turning to prevent burning. Cover with foil and roast in a 180°C (350°F/gas 4) oven until done. Rest the meat for a few minutes before slicing and serving.

You may add some water to the roasting pan to prevent burning. I like to use rump of young lamb in this recipe and cook it only to a medium stage, so it cooks reasonably quickly. However, if you are using a different cut or slicing the meat prior to cooking, adjust the cooking time accordingly. Use desiccated coconut if freshly grated is not available. This marinade is excellent for roasting a whole joint, such as a rolled shoulder of lamb.

I recommend serving this with another classic vegetable dish from Kerala called 'Pulikari' (Pumpkin in tamarind gravy, see recipe page 115). This combines well because its sourness offsets the spicy lamb.

sakarkhand boti

lamb with sweet potatoes

Here is a real twist to the popularly held belief—an Indian curry with NO CHILLIES—and this is truly authentic! This classic dish is from the homes of the Parsis, whose style is unique and simple.

SERVES: 4

4 lamb loin chops

2 large red onions

2 cm (³/₄ in.) piece ginger

5 cloves garlic

¼ cup brown vinegar

800 g (1 lb 12 oz) sweet potatoes

5 cardamom pods

1 cup sugar

2 cinnamon sticks

½ cup oil

salt

extra oil to deep-fry

1 nutmeg

Trim the lamb of all the fat. Slice the onions very finely. Peel ginger and garlic and grind with vinegar into a paste. Parboil the sweet potatoes. Peel and cut them into discs. Dry-roast cardamom and grind into a powder. Heat sugar and 2 tablespoons of water in a pan and cook for 3–4 minutes to make a syrup. Keep syrup warm. Break cinnamon sticks into large pieces.

Heat oil in a pan and add cinnamon stick pieces. Add the sliced onions and fry on a gentle heat, stirring constantly, until evenly browned. Add the garlic and ginger paste and stir. Add the meat and seal well. Add 1 cup of water and a little salt. Bring to the boil and simmer, stirring occasionally, until the meat is cooked and all the water has been absorbed.

Heat more oil in a deep pan and deep-fry the sweet potato discs until golden brown. Drain sweet potato and put into the syrup. Heat the pan with the syrup gently while the sweet potato absorbs all the syrup and becomes soft. Place on a platter, grate nutmeg over it and sprinkle with cardamom powder. Arrange the meat on the sweet potatoes and pour the pan juices over.

Alternatively, you can use diced lamb leg.

The meat and sweet potato can be served together or separately. Any Parsi style bread or rice and vegetables may also be served alongside.

pasanda khada masale ka

sliced lamb with crushed spices

Simple and very quick to prepare, this spicy dish makes an excellent appetiser.

SERVES: 4

750 g (1 lb 10 oz) leg of lamb
5 cloves garlic
juice of 2 lemons
salt
5 cardamom pods
1 tbsp fennel seeds
5 dried red chillies
1 tbsp nigella seeds
2 sprigs fresh spearmint
1 tbsp plain flour
oil to pan-fry

Clean the meat and remove all the fat and sinew. Cut meat into slices of even thickness, then beat them with a mallet to make thin slices. Peel garlic and grind into a fine paste with half the lemon juice and a little salt. Coat the lamb slices with the paste. Dry-roast the dry spices individually over gentle heat and crush them. Pick the mint leaves and chop them, chopping up the stalks as well (separately) if not woody. Mix the mint with the crushed spices and plain flour. Dab the meat slices in this spice mix to coat evenly.

Heat oil in a pan. Fry the meat slices on both sides evenly. Sprinkle with remaining lemon juice.

For ease of preparation, you can use commercially available chilli flakes.
I have tried this recipe with beef and it works just as well. Instead of sliced meat, this mix can be used on larger joints like striploin (after sealing meat first) and roasted. You can also skewer small cubes of meat, then marinate them in just the same way for a snack-style meal.

Serve this with Yoghurt and spinach relish (Duhi palak, see recipe page 183) to offset the chilli heat, with some Tandoori bread (Naan, see recipe page 134) alongside.

khorma chutneywali

lamb with mint chutney

Technically, 'khorma' is a style of cooking where the sauce is cooked until all the moisture dries out and the oil separates from it. But in practice, most chefs reduce the sauce to a thick consistency. This recipe doesn't strictly adhere to the definition of khorma, but gives a very good end result.

SERVES: 4

600 g (1 lb 5 oz) lamb backstraps
salt
½ cup ghee
2 onions
5 green chillies
2 cm (¾ in.) piece ginger
5 cloves garlic
1 bunch fresh spearmint
½ bunch fresh coriander
1 tbsp cardamom pods
½ cup slivered almonds
½ cup yoghurt
¼ cup cream

Trim the lamb and cut into 4 even-sized pieces. Rub with some salt and a spoonful of the ghee and set aside. Dice onions very finely. Deseed chillies and sauté in some ghee. Peel ginger and garlic and grind into a fine paste. Reserve some mint leaves for garnish, then blend together remaining mint leaves, coriander and sautéed chillies. Peel half the cardamom pods and pound into a fine powder. Grind half the almonds into a fine powder in a coffee grinder or any such appliance. Chop the other half of the almonds coarsely. Dry-roast without colouring. Shred the reserved mint leaves and mix with the coarsely chopped almonds. Beat the yoghurt to a smooth consistency.

Heat remaining ghee in a heavy-based pan. Seal the lamb pieces on high heat on all sides then remove. Add remaining cardamom pods and sauté. Reduce heat and add onions. Sauté without colouring. Add the ginger and garlic paste and cook well. Remove pan from heat and whisk in the yoghurt with some water and half the cream. Whisk well and return pan to heat. Season and cook, stirring occasionally. When most of the moisture is cooked out, add ¹/₂ cup of water and cook down again. Add the blended mint mix and almond powder. Whisk, bring to a quick boil, and place the lamb in the sauce. Simmer for 4 minutes or so until the required doneness is reached, and remove.

Set the lamb aside for a minute to drain, and add the juices back into the pan. Roll the lamb in the coarse almond and mint mix. Simmer the sauce and finish off with the remaining cream and the ground cardamom. Slice the lamb and serve with the sauce.

If a different cut of lamb is used, simmer the meat well before adding the almond meal. Once almond meal is added, it tends to get stuck and burn easily.

A very delicately flavoured dish, this would be balanced off with an equally delicate dry vegetable dish from the same region of central India made with baby eggplant called 'Baingan ke lonj' (Baked eggplant, see recipe page 118).

achar gosht

lamb with pickling spices

Each region in North India has different styles of this dish, making the end product look and taste entirely different.
This version is one of my oldest favourites from Delhi.

SERVES: 4

5 onions
1 cm (½ in.) piece ginger
4 cloves garlic
3 cups yoghurt
1 tbsp ground coriander
½ cup vinegar
salt
4 lamb leg chops
1 tbsp cumin seeds
1 tsp black cumin seeds
½ tsp fenugreek seeds
½ tsp nigella seeds
½ tsp black mustard seeds
6 large green chillies
1 cup ghee

Peel the onions. Cut half the onions into chunks. Put chunks into a pan with 1 cup of water, boil until soft, and puree. Slice the other half of the onions. Peel ginger and garlic and puree. In a heavy-based pan mix the yoghurt, garlic and ginger puree, ground coriander, sliced onions, vinegar and some salt. Mix in lamb. Set aside for half an hour to marinate.

Dry-roast each of the spices—cumin, black cumin, fenugreek, nigella and mustard seeds—individually. Crush them individually and mix. (It is important to roast and crush them separately as the flavours would vary drastically otherwise.) Slit the chillies down the centre to form a pocket and fill with the spice mix. Keep any excess spice mix.

Melt the ghee, then add to the meat mix. Bring to the boil and stir. Simmer, stirring continuously. Once the onions are broken down, allow to simmer gently until the meat is three-quarters done. Sprinkle in the chillies and any remaining spice mix. Seal with a tight-fitting lid. Bake in a preheated 180°C (350°F/gas 4) oven for 20 minutes. Remove and rest for a few minutes prior to opening the lid. Gently shake the pot sideways for the spices to blend in. The ghee will have separated. Skim if required.

Although this is authentically prepared as a stew with diced goat, this cut of lamb works really well. Traditionally, this is not a very spicy, hot dish. The black cumin seeds can be difficult to find in regular spice shops (they are called 'shahi jeera', literally 'royal cumin') but can be sourced from Indian spice shops.

I serve this with Stuffed capsicums (Bharwaan simla mirch, see recipe page 108), which is from the same region. With the variety of capsicums now available, choose one that takes your fancy.

chapli kabab

spicy lamb rissoles

Exceptionally versatile, this recipe may be cooked on the barbecue and served as an appetiser or snack.
Traditionally a spicy dish.

SERVES: 4

600 g (1 lb 5 oz) lamb leg meat

1 onion

3 green chillies

3 cm (1¼ in.) piece ginger

5 sprigs fresh coriander

2 dried red chillies

1 tbsp coriander seeds

2 tomatoes

1 egg

2 tbsp unrefined maize flour

salt

oil to pan-fry

Clean and trim the meat; chop very finely or mince very coarsely in a mincer. Finely chop the onion, green chillies (deseed if desired), ginger and fresh coriander (including the stalks). Gently dry-roast and crush the dried red chillies and coriander seeds. Blanch, deseed and chop up the tomatoes. Combine all the chopped vegetables, dried spices, meat, beaten egg, maize flour and some salt. Mix well and rest for half an hour. Divide into 4 equal parts and shape into flattened rissoles.

Heat oil in a pan and pan-fry rissoles until golden brown. Turn over and fry the other side too until cooked through.

You can serve this as a 'lamburger' with some relish sandwiched in a roll. Alternatively, the mix could be put on a skewer and cooked like a 'seekh kabab'. The lamb could also be replaced with beef if required.

The presentation and accompaniments can vary depending on the method of preparation. I use a really great combination from this region—Baked saffron bread (Taftaan, see recipe page 137), a very old traditional Indian bread, and Pumpkin and yoghurt relish (Kaddu ka raita, see recipe page 183).

adraki chaamp

lamb cutlets with ginger

Traditionally this popular North Indian dish is cooked in the tandoor; however, it can be done as well on a grill or a barbecue.

SERVES: 4

8 lamb cutlets

3 cm (1¼ in.) piece ginger

5 cloves garlic

salt

½ cup yoghurt

juice of 2 lemons

2 tsp ground cumin

1 tbsp chilli powder

1 tsp garam masala*

oil to pan-fry

clarified butter to baste

Trim and scrape the bones on the cutlets to clean them. Peel ginger and garlic and blend into a paste. Rub the lamb cutlets with some salt and the ginger and garlic paste, and set aside. Mix yoghurt, lemon juice, cumin, chilli powder and garam masala in a bowl. Add salt to taste. Rub the lamb with this mix and set aside to marinate for a couple of hours.

Roast in a moderately hot tandoor on metal skewers. Alternatively the lamb may be cooked in an oven. To do this, heat oil in a roasting pan and seal the cutlets on all sides. Place in a preheated oven at 190°C (375°F/gas 5) for 7 minutes. Baste with clarified butter and rest before serving. Collect the juices to drizzle on the cutlets.

*The recipe for Garam masala (Aromatic spice mix) can be found on page 190.

Depending on the occasion, this can be made using single cutlets or an entire rack.

While traditionally accompanied by salad (see 'Tandoori' salad, page 127), this may also be served with some vegetables. A simple, home-style potato dish called 'Jeera aloo' (Potatoes with cumin, see recipe page 119) makes a great accompaniment, along with some bread and Mint chutney (Pudhina chutney, see recipe page 178).

daalcha

lamb with lentils

Although this is an unusual combination, it is very traditional to the region of Hyderabad, where this recipe hails from. It is really simple in its preparation, but big on flavour and without a high count of calories!

SERVES: 4

1 cup split yellow lentils

½ tsp ground turmeric

2 cm (³/₄ in.) piece ginger

4 cloves garlic

1 onion

2 tbsp tamarind pulp

4 lamb leg chops

5 cardamom pods

5 cloves

1 cinnamon stick

2 bay leaves

salt

½ cup ghee

1 sprig fresh curry leaves

1 tbsp chilli powder

Wash lentils and soak in water for 2 hours. Drain, then cover with fresh water, add half the turmeric and bring to boil. Skim constantly and cook until the lentils are almost mashed. Peel and puree ginger and garlic. Slice onion finely. Prepare tamarind pulp (see page 9).

Put the lamb into a pan with the whole spices, some salt, the rest of the turmeric and 2 cups of water. Bring to the boil, then simmer and cook gently until almost done. Remove the meat and strain the stock for later use. Heat ghee in another pan and add curry leaves, then the sliced onions. Sauté until the onions turn golden brown. Add ginger and garlic puree and cook well. Add the chilli powder and then the tamarind paste. Add the lentils and stock. Adjust the consistency of the sauce to a soup-like thickness by adding some more water if necessary. Add the meat and simmer until tender. Serve hot.

I use lamb leg chops as the bone adds flavour to the dish, especially since the meat is being poached and the stock used. However, any other cut of lamb that lends itself to slow cooking may be used. Some add 'lauki' (otherwise called 'gourd' or 'long melons') and/or baby eggplant to the sauce while cooking. I have tried squash with equally good results.

raan-e-khyber

braised whole leg of lamb

Khyber is a place in the north-western province of India. 'Raan' means 'thigh' literally, and this celebration dish is traditionally prepared by cooking a whole lamb leg and sharing it around a dinner table. With a highly fragrant but not hot spice mix, this dish is relatively simple to prepare though it has to be cooked slowly.

SERVES: 4

1.5 kg (3 lb) leg of lamb
5 cardamom pods
1 tsp fennel seeds
1 tsp whole mace
1 tsp cloves
3 cm (1¼ in.) piece ginger
6 cloves garlic
salt
½ cup cream
pinch saffron
1 cup yoghurt
2 tsp chilli powder
½ cup oil
juice of ½ lemon
1 tbsp mixed almonds, walnuts, cashews, chopped

Clean and trim the leg of lamb. Cut some gashes on the meat to allow the marinade to penetrate. Dry-roast the cardamom, fennel, mace and cloves gently in a pan until the aroma is released. Cool and grind to a powder in a coffee grinder or similar blender. Peel and puree ginger and garlic. Rub salt and half the ginger and garlic puree into the lamb leg and set aside. Warm half the cream with saffron in it. Whisk the yoghurt with chilli powder, the rest of the ginger and garlic, most of the spice powder (saving some for later), saffron cream, salt and oil. Marinate the leg in this mix for at least 4 hours or overnight in the fridge.

Preheat the oven to 180°C (350°F/gas 4). Place the lamb and the marinade in a roasting pan and roast in the oven for 40 minutes. Turn and baste occasionally. Add some water if required to top up the braising liquid. Cover tightly with foil and finish cooking. The meat is ready when the flesh is tender and falling off the bone.

Remove from the oven; take leg out of the juices. Remove the bone and discard. Place the meat in large chunks on a serving platter. Skim all the oil off the cooking juices and save for garnish. Deglaze the pan with the remaining cream and lemon juice. Strain into a saucepan and bring to the boil, then simmer. Finish off with the remaining spice powder. Strain again and pour over the meat. Garnish with the nuts and a swirl of the fragrant oil retained from the sauce.

The lamb may be presented like a regular roast and sliced for serving, but this must be done carefully, because the meat tends to be very soft and falls apart.

Serve with some dry vegetables such as Fresh corn and greens (Makkai saag, see recipe page 122).

khaas seekh aur saag

'special' minced lamb kebab with spinach

'Seekh kabab', or minced lamb on skewers, is an old classic. 'Saag gosht', or lamb with spinach, is another extremely popular North Indian dish. In this interesting recipe, we have crossed these two for a reason. Read on.

SERVES: 4

700 g (1 lb 9 oz) lean lamb leg
3 red onions
3 cm (1¼ in.) piece ginger
8 cloves garlic
½ red capsicum
5 green chillies
5 sprigs fresh mint
5 sprigs fresh coriander
salt
3 tsp garam masala*
1 egg
400 g (14 oz) English spinach leaves
½ cup oil
1 tbsp chilli powder
¼ tsp ground turmeric
50 g (1¾ oz) butter
¼ cup cream
juice of 1 lemon

Finely chop or coarsely mince the lamb. Peel onions, ginger and garlic. Dice the onions very finely. Grind half the ginger and garlic into a fine paste, and dice the rest finely. Deseed and chop the capsicum and chillies. Finely chop the mint and coriander. Mix some salt, 2 teaspoons of the garam masala, chillies, ginger and garlic paste and the coriander with the lamb. Set aside for an hour. Divide into 8 equal parts and form each into a 10 cm (4 in.) long cylindrical shape and lightly flatten along the length. Beat the egg. Mix capsicum, onions, mint and half the diced garlic in a wide bowl. Dip the kebabs in the egg then roll in the chopped vegetable mix, pressing firmly so it sticks to the meat.

Bring ½ cup of water to the boil in a pan, add a pinch of salt and the spinach leaves. Stir as the leaves wilt. Cook well, drain and refresh in chilled water, then puree finely. Heat oil in a pan. Add the chilli powder, turmeric and the remaining chopped garlic. Add the spinach puree and stir continuously as the spinach tends to splutter. Finish off with butter, cream and remaining garam masala and continue to simmer.

Heat a pan and seal the kebabs on both sides, then place on a baking tray and finish off in a preheated 180°C (350°F/gas 4) oven until the meat is just cooked (about 5–6 minutes). Sprinkle kebabs with lemon juice immediately. Strain the pan juices into the spinach sauce. Place the kebabs in the spinach sauce and simmer for 1 minute. Serve hot.

*The recipe for Garam masala (Aromatic spice mix) can be found on page 190.

Traditionally in Saag gosht, the meat is cooked with pureed spinach so when the lamb is cooked, the spinach is overcooked and discoloured. However, if the spinach is cooked separately and just poured over the lamb, the flavours are not exchanged. This is a happy medium where the spinach keeps its appearance and nutrients, and still absorbs the taste from the lamb.

Although this presents well without much garnish, I like to add a swirl of cream and rogan (oil that separates when cooking lamb in a sauce) and serve it with Maize flour bread (Makkai ke roti, see recipe page 143).

soyta

lamb with creamed corn

Here, I have simplified a traditional recipe from the state of Rajasthan, because of the quality of the produce available today. Fresh corn is very tasty and delicate, and so is the backstrap of lamb. So this reworking of a classic is quicker, lighter and simpler to prepare.

SERVES: 4

800 g (1 lb 12 oz) lamb backstraps
4 tomatoes
½ nutmeg
2 cm (¾ in.) piece ginger
½ cup oil
salt
½ tsp ground turmeric
1½ red onions
5 sprigs fresh coriander
2½ cups fresh corn kernels
1½ tsp chilli powder
2 tsp ground coriander
1 tsp garam masala*

Clean, trim and remove the silver membrane from the lamb backstraps. Divide into 4 equal parts. Blanch and chop the tomatoes. Grate the nutmeg. Peel and grate the ginger. Mix ginger, nutmeg, 1 tbsp oil, salt and turmeric. Rub over the lamb and set aside. Peel onions and chop finely. Pick coriander leaves and chop up the stalks. Chop up the corn kernels roughly.

Heat the remaining oil in a pan and seal the lamb well on all sides, then remove and set aside. Add chopped onions to the pan and sauté. Add the chilli powder and ground coriander and stir well. Add the tomatoes and salt and cook well until the mix is almost in a paste form and the oil separates. Add the corn with all its juices and a little salt. Bring to the boil, then simmer. Stir well. Cook until corn breaks up and the mix is thick like a relish. Place the lamb on top of this mix. Cover and cook for a few minutes until the desired doneness of lamb is achieved. Remove the lamb, then sprinkle the corn mix with garam masala. Stir well, and add some water if necessary. To serve, spread the corn on a plate and top with sliced lamb and a sprinkle of fresh coriander leaves.

*The recipe for Garam masala (Aromatic spice mix) can be found on page 190.

Serve the well-known bread from Rajasthan, Chickpea flour bread (Besani roti, see recipe page 142) alongside.

gosht irani

lamb with vermicelli

A dish from the 'Moghlai' style of cooking, as practised by the cooks of the Mogul rulers. The Moguls came from Persia, of which Iran is a state now. Hence some of the ingredients may seem foreign to Indian cuisine.

SERVES: 4

750 g (1 lb 10 oz) shoulder
    of lamb, boned
salt
2 onions
4 cloves garlic
7 green chillies
½ cup ghee
½ cup milk
½ cup yoghurt
5 cardamom pods
2 tbsp pumpkin seeds
2 tbsp melon seeds
3 tbsp raw cashews
3 tbsp raw peeled almonds
1 sprig fresh mint
70 g (2½ oz) thin vermicelli
½ cup cream
½ tsp garam masala*
1 tsp ground white pepper

Clean, trim and season the lamb shoulder. Roll and tie tightly into a roll. Peel onions and garlic. Slit the chillies and remove the seeds. Sauté chillies in some ghee until soft. Puree the onions, garlic and chillies in a blender with some water. Mix milk and yoghurt with the onion puree and add cardamon and a pinch of salt. Place the lamb in this mix into a pan and add the rest of the ghee; set aside. Mix the pumpkin seeds, melon seeds, cashews and chopped almonds. Save some of the mix for garnish and soak the rest in ½ cup of warm water. Blend into a fine paste. Pick the mint leaves and shred into thin strips for garnish. Crush the vermicelli.

Bring the lamb with the milk mix to the boil. Skim and then simmer, covered. Add some water as required to top up the cooking liquid. When the lamb is almost cooked, remove and set aside. Add the nut puree to the sauce and cook well, stirring constantly to prevent sticking. Add the vermicelli and simmer until soft. Finish off with the cream, garam masala and white pepper. Return the lamb to the sauce and simmer for a few minutes until the sauce coats the meat and it is fully cooked. The sauce is meant to be fairly thick.

To serve, slice the lamb, coat with the sauce and garnish with a sprinkling of the reserved nuts and mint.

*The recipe for Garam masala (Aromatic spice mix) can be found on page 190.

A different cut of lamb suitable for stewing may be used instead.

This dish is mild and rich, with a thick sauce that is very nutty in its flavour. So a light, spicy vegetable dish would complement it perfectly. I use Stuffed okra (Bharwaan bhindi, see recipe page 125) and serve Tandoori bread (Naan, see recipe page 134) alongside.

jungli khara maans

wild salted lamb

While this recipe is from the royal houses of Rajasthan, it was clearly a huntsman's recipe. It is quite simple in its preparation and comparatively light. The finish is almost that of a stew.

SERVES: 4

4 lamb rumps

5 dried red chillies

1 tbsp coriander seeds

salt

2 cm (³/₄ in.) piece ginger

5 shallots

4 cloves garlic

2 carrots

1 cup yoghurt

4 new potatoes

½ cup ghee

4 cardamom pods

3 bay leaves

½ tsp ground turmeric

1 cup fresh peas

½ bunch fresh mint

Trim the rumps. Dry-roast and crush chillies and coriander seeds. Roll the rumps in a mix of some salt and the crushed chillies and coriander seeds. Peel ginger, shallots, garlic and carrots. Dice carrots into pieces about the size of peas. Chop ginger into fine strips. Puree half the shallots with some water then whisk into the yoghurt. Cut potatoes in half.

Heat ghee in a pan. Seal the lamb rumps, then remove and set aside. To the same pan, add cardamom, bay leaves and ginger and sauté well. Add whole garlic cloves and turmeric. Whisk in the yoghurt mix and bring to the boil. Season with salt and simmer for a few minutes. Add the whole shallots and potatoes, simmer for a further 5 minutes. Add the lamb and carrots and simmer for about 10 minutes. Add the peas and finish off with the mint leaves. Skim off any excess ghee that separates.

To serve, slice the rump and present on the vegetables.

I've experimented with using large chunks of lamb, as opposed to rump, and the result is just stunning. The original recipe includes whole chillies in the stew, which I have omitted. So, if desired, add fresh chillies.

With all the colourful vegetables and thin, stew-like gravy, this dish looks very attractive. Serve with fresh flat bread such as Crispy bread (Khasta roti, see recipe page 131).

OTHER MEATS

Not all meats are used equally in Indian cuisine. A vast majority of Indians follow the Hindu religion, in which the cow is considered a holy animal. Hence beef is rarely eaten in India—only by the minority of either non-Hindus or non-conforming Hindus. Similarly, pork is not a very popular meat either. Having said that, there are still popular taste sensations using these meats that have come out of this country. For example, one of the dishes that most people associate with Indian cuisine is 'vin d'alho' (Portuguese for 'wine of garlic'), or what is popularised as 'vindaloo'. This well-known Goan delicacy is traditionally made with pork.

An important period in the evolution of this cuisine is the era of the kings or 'Maharajas' of India, who had a passion for hunting. These kings used and propagated the use of game meat and birds. Although not as popular as other meats, it is worth noting the traditional ways of handling game in Indian cuisine. I have picked a few simple recipes for those who like game meats.

And last but not least, there are offals. There are several old, traditional recipes that use offals, which show that they have been always popular. I have featured a couple of recipes using these in the traditional way.

khad khargosh

baked hare

An old specialty of the warriors of the Rajasthan kingdom, this dish was traditionally cooked in a pit, or 'khad'. Before the warriors headed out to the fields, the game meat, spices and thin chappati-like bread were layered, wrapped up in leaves, put into a hole in the ground and covered with burning charcoal and sand. It was dug out hours later for consumption. This recipe has obviously been updated to suit today's kitchen.

SERVES: 4

700 g (1 lb 9 oz) hare meat

3 onions

3 cm (1¼ in.) piece ginger

4 cloves garlic

¾ cup yoghurt

4 green chillies

8 sprigs fresh coriander

4 potatoes

½ cup ghee

¼ tsp ground turmeric

½ tsp chilli powder

1 tsp ground coriander

pinch salt

juice of 2 lemons

12 chappatis*

Clean the meat and chop up finely or make a coarse mince. Peel the onions and dice finely. Peel the ginger and garlic and blend to a puree. Whisk the yoghurt to get a smooth texture. Remove the seeds from the chillies and chop up. Chop up coriander leaves. Dice potatoes into 1 cm (¹/₂ inch) cubes.

Heat ghee in a pan, add half the onions and sauté until golden brown. Add the ginger and garlic puree and cook well. Add the ground spices and then the meat and a pinch of salt. Brown well and add the potatoes. Cook well, until the oil separates. Add the yoghurt and simmer until the meat and potatoes are almost cooked and the mix is dry. Remove from heat and sprinkle with lemon juice. Sprinkle in the chillies and coriander leaves and mix well.

Divide into 11 parts. Place a chappati on some greaseproof paper or foil, and spread with one part of the mince mixture. Add another chappati and repeat the process until all the meat and chappatis are used up. Wrap up and place on a baking tray. Bake in a preheated 180°C (350°F/gas 4) oven for 15 minutes. Cut into wedges of desired size and serve hot.

*The recipe for Chappati (Flat bread) can be found on page 130.

The hare meat may be replaced with rabbit, beef or goat.

Serve with 'Tandoori' salad (see recipe page 127), Mint chutney (Pudhina chutney, see recipe page 178) and raita.

bheja cutlet

sheep's brain rissoles

A Parsi style delicacy. There are several dishes done with sheep's brains around the country. One unforgettable version was made by a well-known street vendor in Bombay, who would dish out 'bheja tawa masala', and customers would queue up into the early hours of the morning until all the stock ran out!

SERVES: 4

2 sheep's brains
1 onion
2 green chillies
2 sprigs fresh coriander
1 egg
½ tsp ground turmeric
salt
½ cup breadcrumbs
oil to deep-fry

Soak the brains in water for half an hour. Remove from water and clean out, removing the outer skin, blood vessels, etc. if they have not been cleaned already by the butcher. Peel the onion and chop finely. Deseed and chop up the chillies. Chop up coriander leaves finely. Beat the egg.

In a pan, place the brains with turmeric, chillies, onion and some salt, and heat. Do not add any water or oil for cooking. Cook, stirring constantly, until the meat starts to break up and the brains are mashed. Remove from heat and cool. Add 2 teaspoons of breadcrumbs and mix.

Divide into 8 equal portions. Roll and shape as desired, although a heart shape is traditional. Roll in remaining breadcrumbs.

In a pan, heat enough oil to cover the rissoles. Dip each rissole in the beaten egg and fry until golden brown.

It is important to clean out the brains well before cooking.

I like this with salad and the Parsi tomato sauce (see recipe page 185). To turn it into a main meal, serve with some vegetables and potatoes.

bifes assado

roast beef

A classical old Goan recipe. Although the name literally means roast beef, the meat is actually fried! Being rich and spicy, I would ideally serve it with sanna, a steamed rice pudding.

SERVES: 4

800 g (1 lb 12 oz) beef sirloin,
    trimmed
3 onions
3 cm (1¼ in.) piece ginger
5 cloves garlic
2 tomatoes
2 tsp ground cumin
2 tsp gound black pepper
2 tsp ground cinnamon
2 tsp chilli powder
1 tsp ground turmeric
½ cup malt vinegar
salt
1 cup oil

SANNA

2 cups basmati rice
1 x 375 ml (12 fl oz)
    tin coconut cream
30 g (1 oz) dried yeast
3 tsp sugar
½ tsp salt

Cut the trimmed meat into 4 equal-sized steaks. Chop the onions very finely. Peel ginger and garlic and grind into a puree in a blender. Puree the tomatoes. Mix all the ground spices with vinegar and some water to make a smooth paste. Smear some of the spice and vinegar mix and some salt on the steaks and set aside.

Heat half the oil in a pan and add the onions. Sauté well until golden brown. Add the ginger and garlic puree, cook well. Add the spice mix and then the tomatoes, and season with salt. Simmer until the mix is cooked, for another 15 minutes. In a separate pan, heat remaining oil and seal the steaks on both sides. Remove from pan. Deglaze the pan with a little water and add to the sauce. Add the steaks to the sauce and simmer to the desired degree of doneness.

TO PREPARE THE SANNA: Wash rice and soak in water for 4 hours. Drain and put in a blender with the coconut cream and blend to a thick paste. Soak the dried yeast in a little lukewarm water and mix in the sugar. Rest for a few minutes. Mix the yeast mixture with the rice paste and add salt. The batter should be very thick. Cover and leave to ferment for about 4 hours in a warm place.

Grease 4 small dariole moulds or ramekins. Spoon the batter into the moulds and steam for 20 minutes. Cool and remove from moulds.

You can also cook this as a roast: leave the sirloin whole, seal and roast in a roasting pan in a preheated oven at 180°C (350°F/gas 4) for approximately 20 minutes.

Slice the beef and serve with sanna and salad.

karal kurumilagu varuval

liver with pepper

One of our family friends, a fantastic cook of Kerala style food, introduced me to a new delicacy virtually every school holidays! This recipe is for the dish that was my first introduction to offals.

SERVES: 4

500 g (1 lb 2 oz) lamb's liver
1 tsp vinegar
salt
½ tsp ground turmeric
½ tsp chilli powder
6 shallots
3 cm (1¼ in.) piece ginger
4 sprigs fresh coriander
2 tbsp black peppercorns
½ cup oil

Clean the liver, removing the membrane covering it. Slice into thin, even pieces. Dry well on paper towel. Mix vinegar, some salt, turmeric and chilli powder in a bowl and marinate the liver in this mix for a few minutes. Peel shallots and ginger and chop very finely. Chop fresh coriander, including the stalks. Dry-roast and crush the peppercorns. Mix the pepper, ginger, shallots and coriander. Put the liver into this mix.

Heat oil in a pan. When very hot, add the liver slices. Sauté, then turn over and cook the other side.

Sealing the liver on a high heat helps retain the moisture and keep the liver juicy. If preparing large quantities, seal a few slices at a time and return to the pan to finish cooking.

Although this recipe is for liver (or 'lamb's fry', as it is known in Australia) only, it can be made with most offals.

I serve this with a bread very typical of Kerala, called 'Parota' (Layered bread Kerala style, see recipe page 135).

pandi chops

pork cutlets

I acquired this unique recipe many years ago from a well-respected chef and colleague. It is from Coorg, a town in the state of Karnataka, although pork is not the most popular meat in the region. This dish is really simple but very tasty.

SERVES: 4

4 pork cutlets

1 onion

2 cm (³/₄ in.) piece ginger

4 cloves garlic

6 green chillies

5 sprigs fresh coriander

1 tsp cumin seeds

1 tsp black peppercorns

2 tsp white vinegar

salt

½ tsp ground turmeric

1 tsp chilli powder

½ cup oil

Clean the cutlets and trim the bones and the fat, leaving the desired amount of fat. Peel onion, ginger and garlic. Chop chillies and coriander leaves. Lightly dry-roast cumin seeds and peppercorns, and crush. Put all these ingredients (except the meat) in a blender with the vinegar and blend to form a coarse paste. Add some salt, the turmeric and chilli powder. Coat the pork in this mix and marinate for at least 3 hours.

Heat oil in a pan. Seal the pork cutlets on both sides. Reduce the heat and continue cooking. Sprinkle some water along the sides of the pan if the marinade is burning. When the meat is completely cooked, remove from pan. Reduce the pan juices and coat the cutlets with it. Serve hot.

I recommend leaving some fat on the meat and removing it prior to serving if so desired, because it helps keep the meat moist during cooking. The pork could also be cooked on the barbecue.

To offset and complement the dry, spicy pork I serve it with traditional Pineapple chutney (Pineapple gojju, see recipe page 179).

pastelao

meat pie

A true Portuguese-influenced Goan delight, this dish is unique. This is a good example of the use of mixed meats.

SERVES: 4

PASTRY

125 g (4½ oz) unsalted butter
250 g (9 oz) plain flour
1 egg yolk

FILLING

½ tsp ground turmeric
salt
1 tbsp chilli powder
200 g (7 oz) beef topside, diced
100 g (3½ oz) pork neck, diced
100 g (3½ oz) chicken thigh
     fillets, diced
2 Goan sausages
     or hot chorizo sausages
1 tbsp plain flour
2 onions
2 cm (¾ in.) piece ginger
4 cloves garlic
2 tomatoes
2 carrots
2 medium potatoes
2 tbsp ground cumin
2 tbsp ground black pepper
¾ cup vinegar
1 cup oil
1 cup peas

TO PREPARE THE PASTRY: Cut the butter into small cubes. Sift the flour into a bowl and rub the butter in gently to get a crumbly texture. Add 2 tablespoons of chilled water and mix to form a dough. Do not knead the dough too much; handle gently. Rest for 25 minutes under a damp cloth. Divide dough in half, with one half slightly larger than the other, and roll out into two discs. Use the larger one to line a 22 cm (8½ in.) pie tin. Use a fork to prick the pastry. Refrigerate until ready to use.

TO PREPARE THE FILLING: Heat 3 litres (6 pints) of water in a pot. Add turmeric, some salt and 1 teaspoon of chilli powder and bring to the boil. Add the beef, bring to the boil, par cook and remove. Top up the water only if needed. Repeat the process for the pork, chicken and lastly the sausages. Drain stock into a bowl and skim. Cut the sausages into even-sized (roughly 2 cm / ¾ in.) cubes and mix all the meats. Cool the meats and sprinkle with the flour.

Peel onions and chop finely. Peel ginger and garlic and grind into a paste. Puree the tomatoes. Peel and dice carrots and potatoes. Mix cumin, pepper and the remaining chilli powder with vinegar to make a paste.

Heat oil in a pan. Add the onions, cook well and add the ginger and garlic puree. Fry well and add the spice mix. Add the tomato puree and cook until the oil starts to separate. Add the meats and all the stock. Bring to the boil, then simmer for a few minutes. Add the vegetables. Cook until all the meats and vegetables are just cooked, and adjust the seasoning. The finished filling must be fairly thick and dry. Cool thoroughly.

TO ASSEMBLE: Fill the pastry shell with the filling. Cover with the smaller pastry disc and cut holes in the top for steam. Seal the edges well and flute. Brush with beaten egg yolk. Bake in a preheated 180°C (350°F/gas 4) oven until the pastry is well cooked and golden brown.

espetaad

pork chops east indian style

I picked up this very special recipe from an old friend's mother very early in my career in Bombay.
It was the first time I had tasted pork. In those days I considered this recipe to be quite revolutionary.
For a classical Indian recipe, I think it still is different.

SERVES: 4

1 tbsp tamarind pulp
4 pork cutlets
salt
¼ tsp ground turmeric
4 shallots
4 cm (1½ in.) piece ginger
1 tbsp coriander seeds
5 sprigs fresh coriander
1 sprig fresh curry leaves
1 tsp chilli flakes
3 cooking apples
2 tsp ground cinnamon
1 tbsp sultanas
2 tbsp sugar
1 tbsp unsalted butter
½ cup oil
2 tsp chilli oil

Prepare tamarind pulp (see page 9). Trim and scrape the bones of the pork cutlets. Marinate in some salt and the turmeric for half an hour. Peel shallots and ginger. Chop the ginger and one-third of the shallots finely. Dry-roast and crush coriander seeds. Chop the coriander leaves with the stalks, saving some leaves for garnish. Chop the curry leaves into strips. In a bowl, mix crushed coriander seeds, chilli flakes, fresh coriander, ginger, shallots and tamarind pulp. Coat the chops with this mix and marinate for 2 hours. Slice the rest of the shallots into fine, even slices and fry to a golden brown colour. Cool and crush, saving some for garnish. Peel apples and cut into small cubes.

Put the apples, cinnamon, sultanas and sugar in a pan with 2 tablespoons of water. Heat the pan and bring to the boil, stirring occasionally. Cook the apples until almost mashed. Add a pinch of salt and the butter. Mix through well. Add the crushed shallots, simmer until melted into the apple mix and remove pan from heat. Heat some oil in another pan and pan-fry the pork cutlets over moderate heat until browned. Turn over and continue cooking until well cooked. Add the apple mix to the pan. Finish off cooking the pork cutlets in the apple mix to exchange their flavours.

Garnish with reserved crushed shallots and coriander leaves and drizzle with chilli oil.

The apple mix can be used as a relish with other roast pork dishes too.
Deep-fried apple chips make a wonderful garnish.

pal porial

goat with coconut

In this recipe, which hails from the southern state of Kerala, the meat is twice cooked—poached first and then finished off in a pan. 'Pal' (meaning milk) indicates coconut milk, and 'porial' means to fry.

SERVES: 4

16 goat cutlets
1 tsp fennel seeds
5 cardamom pods
2 tsp chilli powder
salt
¼ cup vinegar
½ cup oil
1 sprig fresh curry leaves
2½ cups coconut milk

Clean and trim the bones on the cutlets. Dry-roast the fennel seeds and cardamom and grind to a powder.

Place the fennel, cardamom, chilli powder, some salt and the vinegar in a pan. Add 1 cup of water and mix well. Place the cutlets in the pan and bring to the boil. Simmer gently, preferably covered, until slightly under the desired degree of doneness. Remove from the heat and save the stock.

When ready to serve, heat oil in a pan. Add curry leaves and cook until they splutter. Return cutlets to the pan and brown quickly. Add the coconut milk and any stock from the poaching. Bring to the boil, simmer and adjust the seasoning.

Other cuts of the meat may also be used. This dish is sometimes served for breakfast with a rice flour flat bread called 'Pathiri' (see recipe page 140), in which case the meat is cut up into small cubes (1 cm / ½ in.). The meat is poached the previous night, refrigerated in the liquid and then finished off for breakfast.

nizami nalli khorma

'royal' goat shanks

These shanks of goat, or 'mutton' as it is called in India, are from Lucknow, which was ruled by the 'Nizams' in the yesteryears. Here is a slow-cooked dish that is really aromatic with spices, without being pungent.

SERVES: 4

4 goat shanks

4 onions

4 cm (1½ in.) piece ginger

6 cloves garlic

6 green chillies

1 tsp whole mace

3 cardamom pods

1 cup yoghurt

2 tsp chilli powder

2 tsp ground coriander

salt

pinch saffron

½ cup raw cashews

¾ cup ghee

2 bay leaves

1 tbsp garam masala*

Clean and trim the shanks. Peel onions and slice very finely. Peel ginger and garlic and puree together into a paste. Slice chillies. Lightly dry-roast mace and cardamom and grind to a powder. In a bowl, whisk yoghurt, chilli powder, ginger and garlic paste, ground coriander and some salt. Put the shanks into this mix and set aside for about 2 hours. Soak saffron in some warm water. Chop up the cashews roughly.

Heat ghee in a pan, then add sliced onions and sauté, stirring constantly. As onions change colour, add cashews. When they turn brown, drain the onions and cashews well, reserving the ghee. When the onions and cashews are cool, puree in a blender. Return the ghee to the pan. Add bay leaves and chillies, and sauté. Then add the shanks and yoghurt mix with about 2 cups of water, and bring to the boil. Simmer, stirring occasionally, on low heat until they are cooked. Add the pureed onions, saffron and garam masala. Stir and bring back to the boil. Finish off with cardamom and mace powder.

*The recipe for Garam masala (Aromatic spice mix) can be found on page 190.

Other cuts of meat can be used as well—such as shoulder or diced leg meat. However, having the shank bone gives body to the sauce.

With this highly fragrant dish, the accompaniments I recommend are Pilaf with 'nine gems' (Navarattan pulao, see recipe page 152) and the 'Tandoori' salad (see recipe page 127), along with a garnish of golden brown onions and some mint leaves.

dungari bateyr lasuni

smoked quail with garlic

Simple, and yet very big on flavour. The combination is magical.

SERVES: 4

8 quail breasts
salt
juice of 2 lemons
10 cloves garlic
2 tbsp black peppercorns
½ cup oil
2 tbsp chickpea flour
2 tsp ground mace
1 tbsp chilli powder
2 sprigs fresh mint
1 small piece charcoal
2 cloves
1 tsp ghee

Trim the quail breasts. Sprinkle with salt and lemon juice and set aside. Peel and crush garlic. Dry-roast and crush peppercorns and mace. Heat half the oil, add chickpea flour and cook on gentle heat for 3–4 minutes, stirring constantly. Transfer to a bowl. Add garlic, peppercorns, mace, chilli powder and chopped mint leaves to the chickpea flour mix with some salt. Mix well. Add the quail breasts and coat with this mix.

Heat the remaining oil in a pan. Seal the quail breasts on both sides. Place on a tray and cover with foil. Finish off in a preheated 170°C (325°F/ gas 3) oven for 10–12 minutes. Remove from the oven. Burn the charcoal. Fold back the foil from the tray with the quail and place a small bowl in the centre of the tray. Place the burning charcoal in the bowl. Put the cloves on the charcoal and spoon the ghee over. Re-cover with the foil immediately as the charcoal starts to smoke. Set the tray aside for a few minutes, then remove the bowl and the quail. Deglaze the pan juices with 2 tablespoons of water, strain and use as an accompaniment.

Squab would also work well in this recipe.

Present with a salad, layered bread and the pan juices.

ubla hua maans

poached goat

Truly interesting and truly unique, this recipe from the north-western mountainous region is unlike most others seen in Indian cookbooks. It is very much a home-style recipe, which I learnt from a colleague while working at the Taj Mahal Hotel. I have updated it (only marginally) to simplify the preparation.

SERVES: 4

800 g (1 lb 12 oz) shoulder of
    goat, boned and rolled
4 onions
3 cm (1¼ in.) piece ginger
4 cloves garlic
1 cup yoghurt
6 green chillies
1 tbsp mix of cardamom pods,
    cinnamon, cloves, bay leaves
    and black peppercorns
2 tbsp chilli powder
salt
½ cup ghee
pinch saffron

Prick the meat roll to allow the stock and the flavourings to penetrate. Slice the onions evenly and finely. Separate out the irregular bits or end pieces to use in the stock. Peel ginger and garlic, and crush gently. Whisk the yoghurt to a smooth consistency. Chop the chillies very finely.

Place the meat in a deep pan. Add the whole spices, chilli powder, ginger, garlic and some salt. Cover the meat with water and bring to the boil. Simmer, skimming, until the meat is over half done. Remove the meat and rest. Strain the stock through muslin cloth and set aside for later use. Heat ghee in a pan, add sliced onions and sauté, stirring, until they start to colour. Add the chopped chillies and continue stirring. When onions are brown, drain and cool on paper towel to absorb all the ghee. Save the ghee left in the pan for another dish. Put the onions with the yoghurt into a blender and puree. Return the stock to the pan and bring to the boil. Add saffron and simmer for 1 minute. Then add the onion puree and whisk well. Simmer for another minute. Return the meat to the sauce and simmer until the required degree of doneness is achieved. Take the meat out and reduce the sauce to the desired thickness, adjust the seasoning and strain. Heat when ready to serve. Slice the meat into even, round slices and serve with the sauce.

Try this recipe with lamb, pork or beef, using any cut that is good for slow cooking. Traditionally, cuts of meat from the shoulder or leg are used along with the bones as they add to the flavour of the stock.

hiran ke kofta aftaabi

venison dumplings

The sauce used in this central Indian recipe is extremely popular. 'Aftaabi' is a tomato-based sauce that is sweet, sour, spicy, aromatic, acidic and creamy—all at the same time! I have used cherry tomatoes to enhance that complexity.

SERVES: 4

8 quail eggs
2 cm (³/₄ in.) piece ginger
3 cloves garlic
600 g (1 lb 5 oz) lean venison
   mince
2 tbsp chilli powder
salt
½ bunch fresh mint
450 g (1 lb) cherry tomatoes
3 tbsp butter
½ tsp dried fenugreek
2 tbsp raw cashews
1 tbsp honey
pinch saffron
pinch ground white pepper
¼ cup cream

Hard-boil the quail eggs; cool and shell. Peel and chop ginger and garlic. Put the meat in a bowl with ginger, garlic, chilli powder, some salt and finely chopped mint. If possible, pass the mix through a mincer to obtain a fine and even result. Divide the mix into 8 equal parts. Flatten in the palm of your hand and put a quail egg in the centre. Wrap the meat around the egg and shape it like an egg. Put the cherry tomatoes in a pan with 1 cup of water and some salt. Bring to the boil and crush tomatoes gently with a ladle as they soften. Simmer for about 5 minutes and pass through a sieve. Discard all the skin and return the tomato puree to the pan. Cut butter into cubes. Gently dry-roast the fenugreek and grind to a powder. Chop up the cashews.

Add cashews to the tomato puree and bring to the boil. Gently drop the venison dumplings into the sauce and bring back to the boil rapidly. Reduce heat and simmer gently until the dumplings are just cooked. Take the pan off the heat and remove dumplings with a slotted spoon, carefully draining all the sauce. Put the sauce in a blender and puree. Strain through a fine sieve and return to the pan. Bring back to the boil. Whisk the butter and honey into the sauce. Add the saffron strands and simmer for a couple of minutes. Finish off with the fenugreek, pepper and cream. Return the dumplings to the pan. Serve hot.

Try this recipe with a different meat mince if unable to source venison. Reduce the quantity of cream and/or butter if you like.

To serve, cut the dumplings in half and place on some sautéed baby spinach leaves. Surround with the sauce and garnish with cream and some coriander leaves.

VEGETABLES

When Indians refer to 'vegetarian dishes', it encompasses not just vegetables, but also dishes with 'paneer' (fresh curd cheese, or some call it 'cottage cheese') and legumes too. So the vegetable dishes available are varied and exciting. In fact, the variety of vegetable dishes is only limited by the availability of the main ingredients. Naturally, the kinds of vegetables grown in India are not as easily accessible elsewhere; however, I have seen a major improvement in the availability of fresh, locally grown vegetables in Australia in recent years.

The majority of Indians are vegetarians by choice, for various reasons. So vegetable dishes are usually seen as a main meal, not just an accompaniment. For day-to-day household fare as well as special occasion or restaurant meals, there is an emphasis on vegetables. However, I have suggested the recipes here to be used as accompaniments to the meals in the earlier chapters, in keeping with the concept of this book.

koshumbir

maharashtrian salad

There is a variety of koshumbir done with different vegetables such as cucumber or onions. This version uses carrots.

SERVES: 4

3 carrots
2 green chillies
5 sprigs fresh coriander
1 tbsp roasted peanuts
2 tbsp fresh coconut, grated
salt
1 tsp sugar
2 tbsp oil
1 tsp black mustard seeds
juice of 1 lemon

Grate carrots with a fine grater. Chop chillies and coriander finely. Chop up peanuts. Place the carrots, chillies, coriander, peanuts and coconut in a salad bowl. Add a pinch of salt and the sugar and mix ingredients well. Heat oil in a pan and fry mustard seeds until they crackle. Pour over the salad along with the lemon juice. Toss the salad.

This is best prepared when ready to eat. Adjust the amount of chilli according to taste or the dish it will accompany. This salad makes a good accompaniment to Griddle-fried kingfish fillets (Surmai tawa masala, see recipe page 21).

kumro phool

battered pumpkin flowers

Although this is an uncommon recipe, it is very authentic. It comes from the eastern region of Bengal.

SERVES: 4

8 pumpkin flowers
1 cup chickpea flour
1 tsp nigella seeds
1 tsp black poppy seeds
½ tsp ground turmeric
1 tsp chilli powder
¼ tsp baking soda
salt
oil to deep-fry

Clean the pumpkin flowers and remove the central stem and the pollen stalk. In a bowl, mix the chickpea flour with the nigella seeds, poppy seeds, turmeric, chilli powder, baking soda and a pinch of salt. Add 1 tablespoon of warm oil and enough water to make a thick batter. Whisk to form batter.

Heat the oil for deep-frying. Dip the flowers individually in the batter and deep-fry until golden brown and crisp. Drain, and serve immediately.

The baking soda is optional but it helps the batter to become lighter. If pumpkin flowers are difficult to source, use zucchini flowers.

This dish can be served with Fish in mustard sauce (Shorshe bata maach, see recipe page 22) or can be eaten as a starter with a dipping sauce of your choice.

goan potato chops

mince-filled potato patties

Here is a really delicate potato dish. Although time-consuming to prepare, this is worth a try for a special occasion.

SERVES: 4

500 g (1 lb 2 oz) potatoes
salt
½ onion
2 cm (³/₄ in.) piece ginger
2 cloves garlic
1 tomato
2 sprigs fresh coriander
oil to pan-fry
1 tbsp Goan spice mix*
250 g (9 oz) beef mince
½ cup breadcrumbs

Cook potatoes in salted boiling water. Drain, peel and mash through a fine masher. Peel onion and chop finely. Peel ginger and garlic and grind into a fine paste. Blanch tomato and dice finely. Chop coriander, including stalks.

Heat oil in a pan. Add onion and sauté well. Add the ginger and garlic paste, followed by the Goan spice mix and the tomato. Add some salt and cook well. Add the beef and a spoonful of water. Stir well and cook until dry. Finish off with the coriander. Drain the oil if necessary, and cool.

Divide the potato into four equal parts. Spread some potato in the palm of your hand. Spread some mince over the potato and wrap the potato around it. Flatten gently, then roll in breadcrumbs. Set in the fridge for an hour before cooking. Heat some oil in a sauté pan or a non-stick pan. Pan-fry the patties until golden brown on both sides. Serve immediately.

* The recipe for Goan spice mix can be found on page 184.

Although the beef filling is traditional in Goa, it may be replaced with lamb or any other filling.

These patties make a good accompaniment to the Goan grilled chicken (Galinha cafreal, see recipe page 37). They may also be served by themselves with some salad for a light meal.

vellarikka kootu

cucumber with split yellow lentils

I learnt this unusual vegetable dish from the Chettinad Palace cook. It is quite simple
to prepare and remarkably tasty.

SERVES: 4

1 cup split yellow lentils

½ tsp ground turmeric

2 green chillies

¼ cup oil

4 Lebanese cucumbers

3 dried shallots

1 cup fresh coconut, grated

salt

1 tsp cumin seeds

1 tsp brown mustard seeds

1 sprig fresh curry leaves

Wash the lentils and soak for about 2 hours. Drain and add turmeric, the slit chillies (remove seeds if desired to make the dish milder) and a spoonful of oil. Peel cucumbers and cut into about 4 cm (1½ in.) pieces. Dice shallots very finely. Put the coconut in a blender with a small amount of water and grind into a paste.

Add enough water to cover lentils, bring to the boil, then simmer until they turn soft. Add some salt and the cucumber. Bring back to the boil and add the coconut paste. Heat remaining oil in a pan. Add cumin seeds, followed by mustard seeds and then curry leaves. Add the chopped shallots promptly when the curry leaves crackle. Brown well. Pour this over the lentil mix. Mix gently and serve.

You can also add polished split white lentils (also called white or split 'urad daal') with the shallots if available. It does add to the flavour and texture.

Serve with the Fried fish (Chettinad meen varuval, see recipe page 23).

kizhangu karuvadu varuval

fried potatoes 'like fish'

Here is another simple recipe from the south. Like most other vegetables dishes, this is very easy to prepare.

SERVES: 4

500 g (1lb 2 oz) potatoes
½ tsp ground turmeric
2 tsp chilli powder
salt
4 shallots
oil to pan-fry
juice of 2 limes

Cut potatoes into wedges with the skin left on. Marinate in turmeric, chilli powder and some salt. Peel the shallots and slice finely.

Heat oil in a pan and sauté the shallots. Set aside in a bowl. Fry the potato wedges until cooked, then toss them into the bowl with the shallots. Sprinkle with salt and lime juice. Serve immediately.

The wedges may be baked instead of fried if so desired. I usually use medium-sized desiree potatoes, but I have used kipflers in the restaurant and they work really well. Use any potatoes that are good for frying or roasting.

These can be eaten with some dip, relish or chutney of your choice for a snack, or served with the Pepper chicken Chettinad (Koli melagu varuval, see recipe page 38).

lucknowi baingan

eggplant lucknow style

Although a simple dish, this is very elegant in its presentation and is one of the very popular starters
on the Qmin menu for vegetarians.

SERVES: 4

2 medium eggplants

salt

½ tsp ground turmeric

1 tsp chilli powder

4 tomatoes

2 onions

1 cm (½ in.) piece ginger

5 cloves garlic

3 sprigs fresh coriander

2 cups yoghurt

juice of ½ lime

oil to pan-fry

¼ tsp garam masala*

Slice the eggplants into rounds 1.5 cm ($^2/_3$ in.) thick. Rub with some salt, half the turmeric and chilli powder, and set aside for few minutes. Peel and chop the tomatoes and onions. Peel the ginger and garlic and grind into a paste. Pick and chop the coriander leaves. Remove all the whey from the yoghurt. This can be done in two ways: put the yoghurt in a muslin cloth, tie the top and hang; or place in a strainer (it takes longer in the strainer). When done, place yoghurt in a bowl, add a pinch of salt, the lime juice and some coriander and whisk well.

Pan-fry the eggplant slices until lightly browned on both sides. Place on an oiled baking tray. Heat oil in another pan. Add the chopped onions and sauté well. Add the ginger and garlic paste and cook well. Add the remaining turmeric and chilli powder and then the tomatoes. Season with salt and simmer, reducing the sauce until it thickens. Finish off with garam masala and remove pan from heat.

Spread a little sauce on each of the eggplant slices and cover tray with foil, sealing well on all sides. Bake in a 180°C (350°F/gas 4) oven for about 5 minutes.

Serve topped with the yoghurt mix.

*The recipe for Garam masala (Aromatic spice mix) can be found on page 190.

This can be served as a starter by itself or with a salad for a meal. If served by itself, garnish with some chopped or shredded ginger and coriander. It can accompany the chicken dish from the same region, Chicken in the style of Awadh (Awadhi khuroos, see recipe page 48).

bharwaan simla mirch

stuffed capsicums

With capsicums now available in a variety of colours, shapes and sizes, this makes a great main meal feature at a share-table; not just for the taste, but also for its stunning presentation.

SERVES: 4

¼ cup oil

4 medium capsicums

½ eggplant

1 zucchini

1 potato

1 cup green peas

salt

½ onion

3 tomatoes

2 cm (³/₄ in.) piece ginger

4 cloves garlic

5 sprigs fresh coriander

1 tsp dried chillies

1 tsp coriander seeds

1 tsp cumin seeds

1 tsp black peppercorns

Top and tail the capsicums and deseed. Rub some oil over the capsicums and roast in a 200°C (400°F/gas 6) oven, then peel. Cut up eggplant, zucchini and potato into 1 cm (¹/₂ in.) cubes. Shell peas and blanch in boiling salted water. Chop onion finely. Puree the tomatoes in a blender. Peel ginger and garlic and grind into a paste in a blender. Chop the coriander leaves. Dry-roast the dry spices in a pan on moderate heat and crush with a mortar and pestle.

Heat remaining oil in a pan. Add the onion and sauté well, without colouring. Add ginger and garlic puree and cook well. Add tomato puree and bring to the boil. Add some salt and reduce a little. Add potatoes and simmer until half-done. Add eggplant and zucchini. Simmer for a few minutes until vegetables are just cooked. Add peas, crushed spices and finally the fresh coriander. Remove from heat, drain and reserve excess oil, and cool the mix. Fill the capsicums with this mix. Spoon some of the oil from the vegetables on the capsicums and roast in a preheated 180°C (350°F/gas 4) oven.

Try different types of capsicums for appeal. The filling can be varied too. I have tried Fresh curd cheese (Paneer, see recipe page 190) with pickling spices (see recipe page 68); mushrooms and spinach with the same spice mix as above; or mixed vegetables, with an equally good result.

This can be served at room temperature. I especially like it to accompany the Lamb with pickling spices (Achar gosht, see recipe page 68) to contrast with the yoghurt-based sauce.

beans porial

stir-fried green beans

'Porial' is a style in which different vegetables can be prepared. The most common one is beans.
A popular dish from the south of India.

SERVES: 4

500 g (1 lb 2 oz) green string
    beans
½ onion
2 dried red chillies
¼ cup oil
1 tsp mustard seeds
1 sprig fresh curry leaves
½ tsp ground turmeric
salt
1 cup fresh coconut, grated

String the beans and chop finely. Peel the onion and dice finely. Break the chillies in half.

Heat oil in a wok or a heavy-based pan. Add mustard seeds, curry leaves, chillies and turmeric. Add the beans and a pinch of salt. Stir-fry then cover for a couple of minutes. Add the coconut and stir-fry again until the beans are cooked.

The whole chillies and curry leaves are normally removed before serving. Replacing the beans with cabbage or sliced potatoes also works well.

This can be a light and easy part of any meal. I use it as an accompaniment for Pepper chicken Chettinad (Koli melagu varuval, see recipe page 38).

kaya, payaru mezhukkupurati

stir-fried green banana and snake beans

The style of 'mezhukkupurati' (literally, 'coated in oil') is equivalent to a modern-day 'stir fry'. This is a very home-style vegetable recipe from Kerala, a southern state.

SERVES: 4

2 green bananas
150 g (5½ oz) snake beans
4 shallots
2 dried red chillies
1 sprig fresh curry leaves
¼ cup oil
½ tsp black mustard seeds
½ tsp ground turmeric
salt

Peel bananas and cut into quarters lengthwise. Slice across into small pieces. Top and tail beans and chop into small pieces—about 5 mm (¼ in.) long. Peel shallots and crush in a blender with deseeded chillies and curry leaves.

Heat oil in a wok or a heavy-based pan. Add mustard seeds and cook until they crackle. Add the shallot mix and then the turmeric. Fry the shallots until golden brown. Add the bananas and beans. Season with salt and stir-fry well. Cover and cook for a few minutes, sprinkling some water along the side of the wok to prevent burning. Stir-fry until vegetables are cooked.

Other vegetables such as okra, green beans or potatoes can be prepared in the same style. Cauliflower can be used too; however, it has to be blanched before stir-frying.

The number of chillies can be adjusted to suit taste. A spicy version, as given here, would complement a mild dish such as Duck in coconut sauce (Tharavu moilee, see recipe page 44).

hak

stir-fried kale

Kale is very much a household vegetable in Kashmir. It is called 'karam ka saag' (divine leaf) and is eaten with rice on a daily basis. It is an excellent source of nutrients.

SERVES: 4

450 g (1 lb) kale
4 red chillies
2 tbsp oil
½ tsp mustard seeds
4 cloves
salt
1 tsp garam masala*

Pick, wash and shred the kale leaves. Slit the chillies and remove the seeds.

Heat oil in a wok. Add mustard seeds and cook until they crackle. Add cloves and chillies. Add the kale leaves and stir-fry. Add a little salt and a spoonful of water to prevent it from burning. Continue to stir-fry until leaves are cooked. Finish off with garam masala.

*The recipe for Garam masala (Aromatic spice mix) can be found on page 190.

Traditionally, a lot more water is added while stir-frying and the kale is simmered until well cooked. I like to use tender kale leaves and very little water to keep the dish drier. If kale is unavailable, use Savoy cabbage or English spinach.

I use this dish as an accompanying vegetable with Twice-cooked lamb cutlets (Kamargah, see recipe page 60).

aloo ka bhurta

crushed potatoes

While a staple dish in North India, most parts of India have their own version, varying in its spice mix.

SERVES: 4

450 g (1 lb) sebago potatoes
salt
½ onion
1 tomato
2 green chillies
1 cm (½ in.) piece ginger
2 sprigs fresh coriander
¼ cup ghee
1 tsp cumin seeds
½ tsp ground turmeric
juice of ¼ lemon

Boil the potatoes in salted water until just cooked. Drain, peel and break up without mashing completely. Peel onion and dice onion and tomato. Deseed and chop chillies. Peel ginger and chop finely. Chop coriander leaves.

Heat ghee in a pan and add cumin seeds. Add chopped ginger and chillies, and sauté. Add onion and fry well, without colouring. Add turmeric and then tomato and cook well. Add a spoonful of water and continue cooking. Add the potatoes and season. Mix well. Adjust the consistency with some water, if required. Finish off with lemon juice and coriander leaves.

If sebago potatoes are not available, use any variety of potatoes with a low moisture content that is good for mashing. This mash is not as fine as creamy mashed potatoes, but has a lumpy texture.

A good accompaniment to the Kashmiri lamb shanks (Nalli roganjosh, see recipe page 58), this dish can be served with some daal (lentils) and roti (bread) to make a simple meal.

makkai khumb kadhai

wok-fried baby corn and mushrooms

A 'kadhai' is a traditional wok-like pan used to cook stir-fry style dishes, whether with meat or vegetables. This recipe is slightly different to the usual tomato-based sauce used in kadhai style cooking.

SERVES: 4

250 g (9 oz) button mushrooms

2 onions

2 cm (³/₄ in.) piece ginger

2 green chillies

3 tomatoes

4 cloves garlic

1 tsp cumin seeds

½ bunch fresh coriander

½ cup oil

2 tsp chilli powder

salt

200 g (7 oz) baby corn

Clean mushrooms and cut in half. Chop onions, ginger, chillies and tomatoes very finely. Peel and puree garlic. Dry-roast and crush cumin seeds. Chop coriander leaves.

Heat oil in a wok or pan. Add chopped ginger and chillies, and sauté well. Add the onions and cook without browning, stirring occasionally. Add the garlic puree and cook further. Add chilli powder and then the tomatoes. Add a pinch of salt. Cook on a medium heat until all the moisture is completely evaporated and the oil starts to separate. Drain the oil and reserve. Remove the sauce from heat and set aside.

Heat the reserved oil. Add mushrooms and baby corn, and stir-fry well. Add the sauce and simmer. Finish off with cumin and coriander leaves. Serve immediately.

The base sauce in this recipe is a versatile sauce to have in the fridge. Different meats and vegetables can be stir-fried with it.

This dish can be served simply with some lentils and bread. But I recommend it as an accompaniment for Minced lamb (Kheema, see recipe page 61) and the crispy wholemeal bread called 'Khasta roti' (see recipe page 131).

pulikari

pumpkin in tamarind gravy

A regular household favourite, this recipe is fairly simple but is a very unusual way to cook pumpkin.

SERVES: 4

500 g (1 lb 2 oz) butternut
   pumpkin
1 cup tamarind pulp
3 dried red chillies
1 tsp fenugreek seeds
1 cup fresh coconut, grated
salt
½ tsp ground turmeric
¼ cup oil
1 tsp mustard seeds

Peel pumpkin and dice into 2 cm ($^3/_4$ in.) cubes. Prepare tamarind pulp (see page 9). Slit chillies and remove seeds. Dry-roast chillies in a pan on gentle heat. Separately, dry-roast fenugreek seeds. Dry-roast grated coconut, without browning. When cool, mix chillies, fenugreek and coconut in a blender and grind into a coarse mix, with a little bit of water to aid blending.

Put the pumpkin in a pan with 1 cup of water, the salt and turmeric. Bring to the boil and simmer until the pumpkin is almost cooked. Add the coconut mix and tamarind pulp. In a separate pan, heat oil. Add mustard seeds and cook until they crackle. Pour over the pumpkin mix and cover. Mix and serve.

Some whole red chillies and asafoetida may be added with the mustard seeds to add some zing. Other vegetables such as gourds or squash may be added or substituted if desired.

Serve as an accompaniment to the braised Kerala style Pan-roasted lamb (Irachi ularthiathu, see recipe page 63).

sakarkhand palak

stir-fried sweet potato and spinach

For a vegetable dish by itself, this is really interesting in its taste. As an accompanying vegetable for a spicier meat dish, it works well due to the slightly sweetish taste of the sweet potato and the freshness of the greens.

SERVES: 4

600 g (1 lb 5 oz) sweet potatoes
salt
240 g (8½ oz) baby spinach
2 cm (¾ in.) piece ginger
3 green chillies
¼ cup oil
2 tsp cumin seeds
¼ tsp ground turmeric
½ tsp chaat masala
½ tsp garam masala*

Peel the sweet potatoes and dice into 1.5 cm (²/₃ in.) cubes. Blanch in boiling salted water, drain and refresh in cold water. Wash, drain and dry the spinach leaves. Peel ginger and dice finely. Slit chillies, deseed and chop very finely.

Heat oil in a wok or pan. Add cumin seeds and cook until they crackle. Add the ginger and chillies, and sauté well. Add the turmeric, then the sweet potato. Sauté and add some salt. Add the powdered spice mixes and toss well. Add the spinach leaves. Toss well, and stir-fry until the spinach is wilted.

*The recipe for Garam masala (Aromatic spice mix) can be found on page 190.

The sweet potato may also be blanched by a quick deep-fry in some vegetable oil. However, the method above is a lighter option.

baingan ke lonj

baked eggplant

I used this recipe during my traineeship back in India and it has always remained one of my favourite ways of doing eggplant. The dish hails from the palaces of a Maharaja in central India.

SERVES: 4

450 g (1 lb) baby eggplants
salt
¼ tsp ground turmeric
2 onions
¼ cup ghee
2 cm (¾ in.) piece ginger
1 tsp black peppercorns
2 tsp chilli powder
2 tsp garam masala*
2 tbsp sugar
juice of 1 lemon

Slit eggplants down the centre. Rub with some salt and the turmeric and set aside. Slice onions evenly and very thinly. Fry in ghee and drain, reserving ghee. When cool and crisp, crush the onions. Peel ginger and crush or chop very finely. In a bowl, mix onions, crushed peppercorns, some salt, the chilli powder and garam masala. Spread this mix evenly onto all the eggplants.

Heat reserved ghee in a pan or baking tray and add the eggplants. Cover and bake in a preheated 180°C (350°F/gas 4) oven. Do not add any water. Bake until fully cooked, approximately 10 minutes. Remove from oven. Mix the sugar and lemon juice and sprinkle over eggplants. Drain the excess ghee before serving.

*The recipe for Garam masala (Aromatic spice mix) can be found on page 190.

Being dry, this dish would be complemented by another dish that has some sauce, along with some bread. I use it as an accompaniment to Lamb with mint chutney (Khorma chutneywali, see recipe page 66).

jeera aloo

potatoes with cumin

A true Indian version of sautéed potatoes. It is prepared right around the country in different forms. This recipe is in the North Indian home-style. It is simple, yet is a very effective accompaniment to any meal, especially barbecued meats.

SERVES: 4

500 g (1 lb 2 oz) kipfler potatoes
2 cm (³/₄ in.) piece ginger
2 green chillies
4 sprigs fresh coriander
2½ tbsp oil
2 tsp cumin seeds
¼ tsp ground turmeric
salt

Peel potatoes and dice into 1.5 cm (²/₃ in.) cubes. Peel ginger and chop finely. Slit, deseed and chop chillies. Chop coriander leaves.

Heat oil in a sauté pan. Put in cumin seeds and then ginger. Add turmeric and then potatoes. Sauté, stirring continuously to prevent the potatoes from sticking to the pan. Season with salt, cover and cook for a few minutes in the steam. Finish off with coriander leaves when the potatoes are cooked. Stir well and serve.

If kipfler potatoes are not available, use any potato variety that is low in moisture and ideal for sautéing.

This is a staple potato accompaniment for almost any meal. I use it with Lamb cutlets with ginger (Adraki chaamp, see recipe page 71).

mirchi ka salan

braised chillies

An old favourite from Hyderabad, this recipe always gets attention, just because of what it is. Everyone, even those who can handle a lot of chilli heat, sits and wonders how it would be to eat pure chillies with spices. The trick lies in the selection of chillies to suit the palate.

SERVES: 4

12 large green chillies
½ cup fresh coconut, grated
2 tbsp raw peanuts
1 tbsp sesame seeds
1 tsp cumin seeds
1 tsp coriander seeds
1 onion
3 cloves garlic
1 tbsp tamarind pulp
½ cup oil
1 sprig fresh curry leaves
½ tsp ground turmeric
salt

Slit the chillies and remove the seeds. Blanch in boiling water to remove the pungency. Dry-roast the coconut, peanuts and sesame seeds in a pan until light brown. Cool and blend into a fine powder. Separately, dry-roast the cumin and coriander seeds and blend to a powder. Peel the onion and garlic and finely dice each separately. Prepare tamarind pulp (see page 9).

Heat oil in a pan, sauté the chillies lightly, then drain well and set aside. Into the same oil, add curry leaves and cook until they splutter. Add chopped onions and sauté well until almost turning in colour. Add the garlic and continue to cook. Add the cumin, coriander and turmeric, then the coconut mix. Cook well, stirring all the time to prevent sticking to the bottom of the pan. Add some salt and the tamarind pulp. Bring to the boil, adjust the consistency with some water if required, and then add the chillies. Simmer for a minute then remove from heat. If the oil separates from the sauce, skim off before serving.

Select the chillies depending on the level of heat desired. The chillies are first blanched and then sautéed to remove the pungency. Cut chillies into smaller pieces if so desired. While I have used fresh coconut, use desiccated if fresh is not available—in fact, some of the chefs in Hyderabad prefer desiccated coconut.

Try this as an accompaniment to Chicken cooked sealed (Dum ka murg, see recipe page 47) with a bread of your choice. However, this recipe can also be used as a chilli relish and stored for a while in the fridge and eaten with toast!

repolho e batata

cabbage with potatoes

A Goan home-style dish. It's a simple recipe, yet if executed well it is very effective, not only as an accompanying vegetable, but as a meal in itself.

SERVES: 4

¼ cup split yellow lentils
200 g (7 oz) cabbage
200 g (7 oz) desiree potatoes
4 green chillies
1 red onion
¼ cup oil
1 sprig fresh curry leaves
½ tsp ground turmeric
salt
½ cup fresh coconut, grated

Wash the lentils well and soak, fully immersed in water for at least an hour. When soaked well, drain the water. Shred the cabbage very finely. Peel potatoes and cut into quarters and then into thin slices. Slit chillies and chop finely. Peel onion and slice finely.

Heat oil in a wok or a pan for sautéing. Add the lentils and stir-fry until lightly browned. Add sliced onions and sauté gently. Add the curry leaves and chillies and continue to stir-fry. Then add the turmeric and potatoes, and stir-fry well. Add the cabbage and some salt. Cover and cook for a minute. Continue to stir and cook on a high heat. The mix should be cooked in a few minutes. To finish add the coconut and mix.

The potatoes may be replaced with fresh green peas. The coconut is optional, depending on the other meal components.

This is a good accompaniment to Roast duck with peri-peri (Bathak peri-peri, see recipe page 50). However, this recipe could complement many other dishes too.

makkai saag

fresh corn and greens

A very popular accompaniment. Although the spinach is not typical, any green leafy vegetable in season is used with the corn.

SERVES: 4

4 cups corn kernels
200 g (7 oz) English spinach
5 sprigs fresh mint
2 cm (³/₄ in.) piece ginger
4 cloves garlic
1 tomato
2 tbsp oil
2 tsp chilli powder
1 tbsp maize flour
salt
2 tbsp butter
1 tsp garam masala*

Chop corn gently to break roughly. Wash, drain, dry and shred spinach leaves. Shred mint leaves and mix with the spinach. Peel and puree ginger and garlic. Blanch tomato and puree in a blender.

Heat oil in a pan. Add the ginger and garlic puree. Cook, stirring, without colouring. Add chilli powder and then the tomato puree. Cook well until the oil starts separating. Add the maize flour, stir well. Add the corn and some salt. Stir and simmer until corn is cooked. Sprinkle on some water if required to prevent sticking or burning. Just before serving add spinach and mint; stir-fry. Finish off with butter and sprinkle with garam masala. Stir and serve.

*The recipe for Garam masala (Aromatic spice mix) can be found on page 190.

Replace the spinach with any other greens that are available. A mix of different greens may also be used. Do not cook too far ahead of serving, as the greens could lose colour.

This can accompany Braised whole leg of lamb (Raan-e-khyber, see recipe page 73), among many other dishes.

kacche kele ke kofte

green banana dumplings

This recipe is very popular with vegetarians—not just because it is nutritious, but also it is suitable for the fasting or 'ginger-garlic-free' diets of several disciplines of Hinduism.

SERVES: 4

3 green bananas

1 tbsp raw cashews

1 tbsp sultanas

1½ cups Basic gravy 1*

½ tsp ground turmeric

salt

oil to deep-fry

2 tsp cumin seeds

2 tsp chilli powder

¼ cup cream

1 tsp garam masala^

Peel bananas and cut up into big chunks. Chop up cashews and mix with sultanas. Prepare the Basic gravy and pass through a sieve. Put the bananas in a pan with turmeric, some salt and enough water to just cover. Cover and cook until bananas are soft. Drain any excess water, dry bananas well. Grate or mash up the bananas in a bowl. Heat 1 tablespoon of oil in a small pan. Add cumin seeds and chilli powder. Remove from heat as soon as the cumin seeds splutter. Pour over the banana mix. Mix well and adjust the seasoning.

Divide banana mix into 12 equal parts. Roll each portion in the palms of your hands into a ball shape and then flatten. Place some cashew and sultana mix in the centre and roll the mix over it. Roll tightly and shape into croquettes. Deep-fry in hot oil and set aside.

Bring the Basic gravy to the boil. Add cream and finish off with garam masala. Adjust the seasoning and simmer to thicken slightly. Serve the dumplings coated with the sauce.

*The recipe for Basic gravy 1 (Tomato-based gravy) can be found on page 186. For Garam masala (Aromatic spice mix) see page 190.

Although this recipe can agree with Hindu diets, I have used the Basic gravy 1 for the sauce, which has ginger and garlic. However you could use the Butter sauce (Makhni, see recipe page 185) to avoid these ingredients.

I like to serve the dumplings on a plate, coated with the sauce and sprinkled with cream, cashews, sultanas and green banana crisps.

bharwaan bhindi

stuffed okra

Okra, or 'ladies fingers' as it is popularly known, is one of the most favoured vegetables among most Indian communities. This particular recipe is from the north of the country and is one of my favourites.

SERVES: 4

650 g (1 lb 7 oz) okra
2 cm (³/₄ in.) piece ginger
3 cloves garlic
2 tsp cumin seeds
1 tsp fennel seeds
1 tsp fenugreek seeds
½ tsp nigella seeds
5 sprigs fresh coriander
¼ cup oil
2 tsp chilli powder
2 tsp dried mango powder
1 tsp garam masala*
salt

Cut tops and tails off okra and make a slit along the length. Peel ginger and garlic and chop very finely. Dry-roast and crush cumin, fennel, fenugreek and nigella seeds. Chop coriander leaves finely.

Heat oil in a sauté pan. Add ginger and garlic, and sauté well. Add all the spices and coriander leaves. Add a pinch of salt and remove from heat. Cool. Fill okra with the mix, and lay the okra on a baking tray, sprinkling any remaining mix on top. Spoon the oil over as well. Bake in a preheated 180°C (350°F/gas 4) oven for about 12 minutes, stirring occasionally. Serve hot.

*The recipe for Garam masala (Aromatic spice mix) can be found on page 190.

The okra may also be cooked in a pan.

I like this with Lamb with vermicelli (Gosht Irani, see recipe page 78). However, this recipe also complements other dishes that are less spicy or creamy. Just add some bread and Pumpkin and yoghurt relish (Kaddu ka raita, see recipe page 183).

kosambari

mung bean salad

Originally from the Coorg region of the state of Karnataka, here is an excellent salad or accompaniment that is simple, delicious and nutritious. While it is authentically prepared with split mung beans that are soaked, I have used mung bean sprouts, which are readily available.

SERVES: 4

450 g (1 lb) mung bean sprouts
2 tbsp split yellow lentils
2 Lebanese cucumbers
2 green chillies
5 sprigs fresh coriander
1 tbsp oil
1 tsp mustard seeds
½ cup fresh coconut, grated
salt
juice of 1 lime

Wash mung bean sprouts and drain. Wash yellow lentils and soak in water for at least 2 hours, then drain. Peel and deseed the cucumbers and dice evenly into 5 mm (¼ in.) cubes. Chop chillies very finely. Chop coriander leaves finely.

In a salad bowl, mix the beans and lentils. Heat oil in a small pan. Add mustard seeds and cook until they crackle. Add chillies and pour the mix over the mung bean sprouts. Add coriander, coconut, cucumbers, a pinch of salt and lime juice, and toss well. Serve immediately.

Add the salt, lime and cucumbers just prior to serving. If prepared in advance, the cucumbers release liquid upon reacting with the dressing, making the salad watery.

A good accompaniment to any dish from this region.

'tandoori' salad

salad for grills

As the name implies, this is a simple salad that can accompany most warm starters right across the country. It has all the elements of what Indians like eating with tandoori kebabs.

SERVES: 4

3 red onions
2 green chillies
2 spring onions
3 red radishes
½ white radish
1 tsp chaat masala
salt
juice of 1 lime

Peel onions and slice into wafer-thin rings (on a slicer if possible). Slit and deseed chillies and cut into fine strips. Separate the green and white parts of the spring onions and slice into very fine strips. Peel red and white radishes and cut into matchstick-sized strips. Wash the onion and spring onion and soak separately in cold water for half an hour. Drain and repeat at least once.

In a salad bowl, mix all the salad vegetables. Add some chilled water and ice and leave to soak for about an hour or place in the refrigerator. Drain and remove all the water by spinning in a salad spinner or drying on paper towel. Sprinkle with chaat masala, salt and lime juice and serve immediately.

You can add tomatoes or cucumbers or any such salad vegetables you like.
Use as an accompaniment for any snacks or grills.

BREADS

Here is a topic that is really exciting to share information about.

Until recently it was unthinkable to see any Indian bread on supermarket shelves. The reason is simple: Indian breads are made fresh and eaten immediately. For most people around the world, the first thing that springs to mind about Indian breads is 'naan', and maybe the 'tandoor'—the charcoal-fired clay oven in which naan is cooked. To make naan, the flattened dough gets slapped onto the wall of the oven. Those specialised in this type of cooking are true artists. However, it is interesting to note that only a small minority of Indians own tandoors!

Bread is a staple in the diets of most Indians and there are innumerable varieties of Indian breads. 'Roti' is almost synonymous with 'meal'. So, breads are made not just in tandoor ovens, but more often on griddles, in earthenware pans, iron ovens and pans. They are made with different flours such as plain, wholemeal, maize, corn, rice or millet. They can also be classified by the way they are made—flat, rolled, filled or layered—or by the region they come from. In fact, given all of these different types and classifications, the topic of Indian breads has the making of a whole cookbook.

But for now, I have listed just a few breads and you can experiment with the varieties that are possible from these.

chappati

flat bread

Chappati has got to be the 'national' bread. Although known by different names such as 'fulka' or 'rotli' and made with slightly different techniques, basically it is wholemeal flat bread. In regions of India where bread is the staple, chappatis are eaten in most households with every meal.

SERVES: 4

500 g (1 lb 2 oz) fine wholemeal flour
salt
water

Place flour and a pinch of salt in a bowl. Make a well in the middle of the flour and pour in water as required, mixing gently to form a dough. Let dough rest for roughly 15 minutes and divide into 8 equal parts. Flatten and roll out into thin discs, about 3–4 mm ($^1/_8$–$^1/_6$ in.) thick. Use some flour for dusting.

Heat a pan or griddle. Place the bread on the pan until tiny bubbles start to appear and it starts turning golden brown. Flip and cook the other side.

This is a good bread for making wraps. They can be kept in an airtight container to prevent drying out, and can be reheated very gently for a few seconds in a microwave immediately prior to serving. The well-known roti is made with a similar dough. Make the dough stiffer by adding less water, and when rolling the dough, leave it thicker. Roti is traditionally cooked in the tandoor and hence called 'tandoori roti'.

khasta roti

crispy bread

A North Indian style bread made with wholemeal flour and flavoured with cumin seeds.

SERVES: 4

1 tsp cumin seeds
225 g (8 oz) wholemeal flour
salt
1 egg
150 ml (5 fl oz) milk
30 g (1 oz) ghee

Dry-roast cumin seeds and crush. Mix with flour and add a pinch of salt. Beat egg and milk in a bowl. Mix the flour with the egg mixture to form a dough. Knead well into a stiff dough and rest, covered with a clean damp cloth. Divide into 8 equal parts. Form into balls and rest again for a few minutes. Flatten and roll out into discs, using some flour to prevent sticking.

Prick the bread with a fork to prevent puffing. Cook on a pan over low heat. When one side is par-cooked, turn over and start the other side. Repeat the process until both the sides are cooked well, and the texture is crispy. Brush with melted ghee.

Some people use semolina while rolling the dough out to get the crispy texture.

Usually served with North Indian dishes, this bread also makes an ideal snack when cut into pieces and served with a dip. I use this bread to accompany the Minced lamb (Kheema, see recipe page 61).

laccha paratha

layered bread

There are several types of layered breads, prepared with different doughs. This recipe is one of the basic versions and yet is really delightful when eaten fresh from the oven.

SERVES: 4

560 g (1 lb 4 oz) plain flour

1 tsp baking powder

salt

1 tbsp sugar

1 egg

150 ml (5 fl oz) milk

150 ml (5 fl oz) warm water (approx)

80 ml (2⅔ fl oz) oil

150 g (5½ oz) clarified butter

Sift 400 g (14 oz) of the flour with baking powder into a bowl, add a pinch of salt and the sugar. Beat egg and milk together. Add milk mix and some water to the flour to form a soft and pliable dough. Knead well and set aside for half an hour under a damp cloth. Knead in oil and rest for a further 20 minutes. Divide into 8 equal portions and form into smooth balls. Spread each portion out into a thin pancake-like sheet, using some flour to dust. Brush clarified butter over this and sprinkle with more flour. Gather bread into concertina folds, like in the making of a paper fan. Roll the gathered bread into a circle to resemble a raisin Danish roll. Set aside for few minutes.

Flatten bread only on one side to preserve the layers. This is usually done by pressing the bread down with your palms on the workbench. Flatten to an even disc 5–8 mm (¼–⅓ in.) thick. Cook in the tandoor or on a preheated oven tray in a 180°C (350°F/gas 4) oven until cooked. As soon as the bread is out of the oven, brush with some melted clarified butter, then place your hands on either side and crush very gently (almost in a clapping motion) to separate the layers.

Literally 'laccha paratha' means 'layered bread'. Paratha can be made with wholemeal flour as well. There are several techniques of creating the layers. The one explained above is simple and effective.

As it is, this paratha works well with any meal. You can also mix some herbs or spices with the dough or sprinkle them in its layers to add flavour and interest.

naan

tandoori bread

Originating in Persia, naan is now the most popular Indian bread worldwide.

SERVES: 4

450 g (1 lb) plain flour

1 tsp baking powder

salt

1 tsp sugar

1 egg

150 ml (5 fl oz) milk

150 ml (5 fl oz) warm water
(approx)

80 ml (2²/₃ fl oz) oil

1 tsp nigella seeds

50 g (1¾ oz) clarified butter

Sift flour with baking powder into a bowl, add a pinch of salt and the sugar. Beat egg and milk together. Add the milk mix and some water to the flour to form a soft and pliable dough. Knead well and set aside for half an hour under a damp cloth. Knead in the oil and rest for a further 20 minutes. Divide into 8 equal portions and form into smooth balls. Set aside for few minutes before cooking.

Take one of the dough balls and place a pinch of nigella seeds on top. Dip in a little oil and rub oil on top of the dough as you flatten it. Using your hands, spread the dough out to an even thickness, about 5 mm (¹/₄ in.). Traditionally naan is shaped into a long triangle and cooked in the tandoor oven. Alternatively, naan may be cooked on a preheated baking tray in a 180°C (350°F/gas 4) oven for about 8–10 minutes. When cooked, brush with clarified butter.

A lot of variations are possible once basic naan dough is prepared. The dough may be topped with almonds, garlic, herbs or spices before cooking. Or it may be filled with a variety of fillings such as potatoes, minced lamb, paneer, vegetables, nuts or fruits and then flattened and cooked.

While naan is a standard bread with most meals, it can also be served with dips for starters too. Try it with the Sliced lamb with crushed spices (Pasanda khada masale ka, see recipe page 65).

parota

layered bread kerala style

For this simple griddle-cooked flat bread from the southern state of Kerala, a good result depends more on its preparation and layering than on the cooking.

SERVES: 4

400 g (14 oz) plain flour
½ tsp salt
200 ml (7 fl oz) oil
hot water

Sift the flour into a bowl, then add salt and 1 tablespoon of oil. Add enough hot water to form a soft and pliable dough. Knead well. Rub the surface with a little oil and rest for half an hour in the bowl under a damp cloth. Divide into 8 equal portions. Roll into balls, cover with the cloth again and rest for a further 15 minutes. Oil a flat surface (preferably marble) to roll out the dough. Roll out with a rolling pin into a circular shape that is paper thin. Spread with some oil and gather up into concertina folds, like in the making of paper fan. Holding one end, wrap the dough around in a spiral and tuck in the end at the bottom. Once again, cover with a damp cloth and rest for a few minutes until ready to cook.

Heat a pan or griddle. Flatten the prepared bread with the palms of your hands or with your fingers into an even disc roughly 10–12 cm (4–4 ³/₄ in.) in diameter. Cook on moderate heat until golden brown. Turn over and cook the other side. When 3 or 4 of these are cooked, place them one on top of the other, then place your hands on either side and crush very gently (almost in a clapping motion) to separate the layers.

The more skilled or experienced cooks spread the bread by holding the rolled dough with both hands and gently throwing it on an oiled surface with a rotating motion to make the bread paper thin. This requires some practice.

A good accompaniment to most dishes from Kerala. I like to serve Parota with Liver with pepper (Karal kurumilagu varuval, see recipe page 86).

taftaan

baked saffron bread

Here is a classic bread. It comes from the northern provinces in the olden days of the Maharajas.

SERVES: 4

500 g (1 lb 2 oz) plain flour
1 tsp baking powder
5 g (1/8 oz) dry yeast
½ tsp ground cardamom
salt
1½ tsp sugar
175 ml (5¾ fl oz) milk
1 egg
150 g (5½ oz) ghee
pinch saffron
¼ cup cream

Sift flour with baking powder into a bowl. Soak yeast in some warm water for a few minutes. Add it to the flour with cardamom and some salt. Prepare sugar syrup by heating 75 ml (2 1/2 fl oz) water with the sugar until sugar dissolves. Mix the milk with the sugar syrup. When cool, mix in the egg and whisk. Add to the flour mix and knead well, until you get a soft dough. Let dough rest under a damp cloth for half an hour. Melt 100 g (3 1/3 oz) ghee and knead in well. Rest in the refrigerator for an hour, covered with a damp cloth. Soak the saffron in warmed cream. Divide the dough into 8 even portions and roll into balls. Dust with flour and roll each ball out like a pizza base into a disc 5–8 mm (1/4–1/3 in.) thick. Rest for a further 15 minutes in the fridge.

Prick all over the bread with a fork to prevent bubbling. Place on a baking tray and cook in a preheated 180°C (350°F/gas 4) oven until golden on the surface. Brush with remaining ghee and saffron cream while still hot out of the oven.

Adjust the shape and size according to the desired use. You can reduce the amount of ghee brushed on after baking if you want to reduce the fat content. This bread can be prepared in advance and stored in an airtight container.

An excellent bread to go with any North Indian style meal, or a good accompaniment for barbecues or as a starter with dips.

bhakri

sorghum flour bread

Traditional and popular in the state of Maharashtra in the west, this bread is not only nutritious, but huge on taste.
It is made with 'jowar', or sorghum flour. Considered peasant food by some, this bread is a staple for many in the region.
It can be a meal in itself, with just some pickles, let alone any vegetables or meat!

SERVES: 4

250 g (9 oz) sorghum flour
salt
water

Mix the flour with some salt in a bowl. Spread the flour to make a well in the centre. Add water as required, a little at a time and mix well to prepare a fairly stiff dough. Rest for a few minutes covered with a damp cloth. Divide into 8 equal parts and form into balls in your palms.

Flatten each dough ball into an even, flat disc about 5 mm ($^1/_4$ in.) thick. Heat a griddle or a non-stick pan. Cook the flattened dough gently and then turn over and cook the other side. Repeat the process until the dough is well cooked. To help the bread puff up, you can press down on the centre and lift off gently with a scrunched cloth while the bread is cooking.

Many people prepare bhakri with some cumin seeds or carom seeds and minced onions and chillies mixed in with the dough, especially if the bread is to be eaten by itself or with a dip. I have kept the bread plain here, which is suitable for serving with a highly spiced and fragrant dish such as Chicken cooked with 'dry' spice (Kombdichi sukhe, see recipe page 55). Sorghum flour can be found in some health food stores or Indian grocers. If unavailable, try this recipe with wholemeal flour (although the result is entirely different).

ragi roti

millet flour bread

A traditional flat bread from the region of Karnataka. Millet, or 'finger millet' as it is known,
is highly nutritious and has no gluten.

SERVES: 4

2 green chillies
4 fresh curry leaves
30 g (1 oz) fresh coconut, grated
1 cup water
salt
250 g (9 oz) millet flour
30 ml (1 fl oz) oil

Deseed chillies and chop finely. Shred the curry leaves. Put the coconut, curry leaves and chillies in a blender and puree well. Transfer puree to a bowl and add water. Add a pinch of salt, then add flour slowly, mixing all the time to form a smooth dough and to prevent lumps. Use up all the flour, adding more water if needed. The dough has to be soft and pliable in the end without being sticky.

Divide the dough into 8 equal parts. Roll into balls in the palms of your hands. Flatten each dough ball on a flat surface (preferably marble) with a rolling pin, using some flour to prevent sticking. Alternatively sandwich in sheets of cling wrap to prevent sticking and roll out into discs about 3–4 mm (^{1}/$_8$–^{1}/$_6$ in.) thick. Cook on a heated griddle or pan. Spoon oil around the sides of the bread. When half cooked, flip like a pancake and cook the other side. When evenly cooked on both sides, remove from the pan and serve hot.

Millet, or 'ragi', can be found in health food stores or some Indian grocers. Substitute with rice flour if it is unavailable. This dough (whether millet flour or rice flour is used) can also be made by the hot dough method as explained in the recipe for Pathiri (Rice flour flat bread, see recipe page 140) for a better result. If using this method, ragi flour can be mixed with some cold water before adding it to the boiling water to prevent lumps from forming in the dough.

This bread is great with Fried chicken from Coorg (Coorgi chicken, see recipe page 54). However, it could accompany many other dishes from this region.

pathiri

rice flour bread

Here is another recipe from the southern state of Kerala. This bread is sometimes eaten for breakfast and is also an ideal accompaniment for any other meal.

SERVES: 4

2 shallots

1 tsp cumin seeds

100 g (3⅓ oz) fresh coconut, grated

300 ml (10½ fl oz) water

pinch salt

300 g (10½ oz) rice flour

Chop the shallots very finely. Dry-roast cumin seeds and grind to a powder. In a blender, combine coconut, shallots and cumin, and puree. Boil salted water in a pan. Add the coconut mix and the rice flour. Using a wooden spoon, stir well. Turn out onto a lightly oiled surface or a flat plate. Knead well while still warm. Divide into 12 equal parts and form into balls. Cover with a damp cloth to prevent drying.

On a lightly oiled surface, flatten each ball with a rolling pin into an even, round shape about 3–5 mm (⅛–¼ in.) thick. Cook on a flat griddle or non-stick pan. If lifting the flattened dough is difficult, line the rolling surface with a lightly oiled banana leaf. Place the dough ball on it. Cover with cling wrap and roll to flatten. When the desired thickness is reached, lift off the cling wrap and invert bread into the pan.

Select the rice flour for this bread carefully to ensure there are no additives. In some parts of the state, the bread is made with just the rice flour and water. The coconut, shallots and cumin are optional. Traditionally these are cooked in an earthenware pot called a 'chatti', which imparts a unique flavour.

Ideally, this bread is served with sweetened fresh coconut extract. Try it with the South Indian Chicken stew (Ishtoo, see recipe page 51).

besani roti

chickpea flour bread

A classic from central India. This bread can be eaten by itself as a snack or to accompany a main meal.

SERVES: 4

1 onion
3 sprigs fresh coriander
100 g (3½ oz) chickpea flour
150 g (5½ oz) wholemeal flour
½ tsp ground turmeric
½ tsp chilli powder
salt
1 tbsp yoghurt
water
40 g (1½ oz) ghee

Peel onion and chop very finely. Chop coriander leaves finely. In a bowl, sift the flours together and mix in turmeric, chilli powder, salt, onion, coriander and the beaten yoghurt. Mix in some water gradually to form a firm yet pliable dough. Let the dough rest, covered with a damp cloth for half an hour. Divide into 12 equal parts. Form into balls in the palm of your hand.

Roll each of the balls of dough into a disc about 3 mm (⅛ in.) thick. Heat an iron griddle or a non-stick pan. Place dough on the griddle. Turn over as the dough starts to blister with the heat. Repeat the process until the dough is fully cooked. Spread a tiny blob of ghee on each bread.

It is important to add some wholemeal flour to the chickpea flour because otherwise it doesn't form into a firm dough (due to the lack of gluten). This quantity can be adjusted to suit individual needs. This bread can be fluffed up on the griddle by using a tea towel to press down and lift off gently as it is cooking. It may even be fluffed up very quickly by placing it on a direct gas ring flame; however, this has to be very carefully executed.

Try it with Lamb with creamed corn (Soyta, see recipe page 76). It can be served as a snack with a yoghurt dip too.

makkai ke roti

maize flour bread

Very typical of Punjab in the north of India, this bread is very tasty and nutritious. Makkai ke roti and a dish of mustard greens and spinach (called 'sarson ka saag') are like the yin and yang of Punjabi food.

SERVES: 4

250 g (9 oz) maize flour
50 g (1¾ oz) white radish, grated
water
salt
1 tbsp oil
50 g (1¾ oz) butter

Mix maize flour with radish and a pinch of salt in a bowl. Add water, a little at a time, and mix well to form a fairly stiff dough. Rub the oil over the dough and rest for half an hour, covered with a damp cloth. Divide into 8 portions. Form into balls in your palms.

Flatten each dough ball and roll with a rolling pin to form a disc about 4 mm (¹/₆ in.) thick. Dust with flour or use some oil on the surface to prevent sticking. Alternatively, sandwich the flattened dough ball in cling wrap and roll out. Place on a heated griddle or a non-stick pan and cook. When slightly cooked on one side, turn over and cook the other side. Repeat the process until both sides are well cooked. Smear with a blob of butter and serve immediately.

Although this bread is literally translated as 'corn bread', cornflour is a very refined, white product that is not appropriate for this recipe. Hence I use maize flour, which is more nutritious and better suited. A coarse corn meal or a fine polenta are close alternatives.

Serving this bread hot with mustard greens and Black lentils with kidney beans (Mah di daal makhni, see recipe page 188) is a sure way of winning friends among Punjabis! Or, try it with 'Special' minced lamb kebab with spinach (Khaas seekh aur saag, see recipe page 75).

RICE

Rice is predominantly the basis of the diet for South Indians. However, rice is grown and eaten right around the country. A variety of different rice grains are grown, the most popular being the white long grain rice (especially the basmati variety). There are also several types of raw rice and brown rice that are eaten in mostly rural parts of India. Wild rice is also available in several parts of the country.

Rice is considered a holy grain among the Hindus. On auspicious occasions rice often features in some form, as an offering to the gods or as part of the religious ceremonies. For example, in the south of India, the harvest festival of 'Pongal' is celebrated with several types of rice dishes—sweet, savoury or spicy—which are made on the day.

The few rice dishes I have selected here demonstrate the different techniques in cooking rice. Rice cooking, which I believe is a skill in itself in this cuisine, can be done in two ways: by boiling (using an excess amount of water and draining) or by absorption (using the correct amount of water for the rice to absorb and cook). It can then also be flavoured (tossing cooked rice with other ingredients).

chawal

boiled rice

Rice is the staple for many and is a standard inclusion in almost all Indian meals. I thought a few simple tips for cooking rice were worth mentioning.

SERVES: 4

4 cups basmati rice
salt (optional)
lemon juice (optional)

Wash the rice to remove all the starch. Drain and then soak in enough water to cover the surface for about half an hour.

Boil approximately 3 litres (6 pints) of water in a pot that has enough room for the rice to cook, as the grains expand to nearly double the size. Add some salt and a little lemon juice if desired. Drain rice and put into the boiling water. Bring back to the boil quickly, stirring gently. The grains are delicate and every effort should be made to prevent them from breaking. Allow rice to boil and turn over in the water for about 6 minutes. Check for doneness by taking a grain and pressing it between the fingers. If there is no white grain left in the centre, the rice is cooked. Drain in a colander. Toss the rice periodically to let the steam escape and prevent further cooking. When fully drained, the rice is ready to serve.

Other types of rice, such as brown and raw rice, can be cooked in the same way; however, these other grains require a longer cooking time. By adding spices or vegetables to flavour the boiling water, the rice can be flavoured too.

parsi kitchdi

rice and lentil mix parsi style

Kitchdi is traditionally a dish of rice and lentils cooked together (and generally overcooked) and is made in many regions. The type of rice and type of lentils vary from place to place and therefore so do the flavours. Here is the Parsi version.

SERVES: 4

1 cup split red lentils

2½ cups basmati or white
   long-grain rice

2 onions

2 green chillies

2 cm (³/₄ in.) piece ginger

3 cloves garlic

¼ cup oil

2 bay leaves

1 tsp black peppercorns

½ tsp ground turmeric

salt

Mix lentils and rice and wash thoroughly until water runs clear. Cover with water and soak for at least half an hour. Peel and chop onions. Slit chillies. Peel ginger and garlic and blend into a puree.

Heat oil in a pan. Add bay leaves and peppercorns. Add onions and sauté without colouring. Add the ginger and garlic puree. Cook well and add turmeric. Drain rice mix and add to the pan, along with the chillies. Stir well and add enough water to cover the rice. A rule of the thumb for the quantity of water is 1 cup of rice to 1¹/₂ cups of water, but that totally depends on the type of rice and how much soaking it has had. Stir occasionally, and add some salt. Bring to the boil, cover and cook on low heat until all the moisture is absorbed.

This is a 'plain' kitchdi, but there are other types such as vegetable kitchdi (with a mix of vegetables and coconut) or a lamb version.

Ideally, kitchdi is served with any yoghurt relish. It makes a great accompaniment to Fish with green chutney in banana leaves (Patra-ni-macchi, see recipe page 16).

elumikkai sadam

lemon rice

There are several renditions of this dish from the southern state of Tamil Nadu. I've chosen a simple one.

SERVES: 4

4 cups basmati rice

5 mm (¼ in.) piece ginger

2 dried red chillies

2 tbsp oil

1 tsp black mustard seeds

1 tsp split yellow lentils

1 sprig fresh curry leaves

½ tsp ground turmeric

1 tbsp raw peanuts

juice of 1½ lemons

salt

Wash, soak and boil rice as described in the Boiled rice recipe (Chawal, see page 146). Peel ginger and chop very finely. Cut chillies in half.

Heat oil in a pan. Add the mustard seeds. When they splutter, add chillies and lentils. Add curry leaves, turmeric, chopped ginger and peanuts. When the lentils and peanuts are golden brown, take pan off the heat and add lemon juice. Pour mixture over the rice in a bowl with some salt and toss well until the rice is coated with the mix and turns an even yellow colour.

Some prefer to add chopped fresh chillies to the oil instead of the dried chillies. The dried chillies could be removed before serving if desired. There are several variations of cooked rice tossed with a flavouring—it's worth experimenting with your favourite flavour.

While this dish is usually prepared for a special occasion as a part of a spread, it works particularly well with Pepper chicken Chettinad (Koli melagu varuval, see recipe page 38).

jeera pulao

cumin pilaf

Here is an example of a simple 'pilaf' style rice—better known as 'pulao' in India.

SERVES: 4

4 cups basmati rice
½ onion
¼ cup ghee
2 tsp cumin seeds
salt

Wash rice and soak for half an hour. Slice onion.

Heat ghee in a pan. Add the cumin seeds and then the sliced onion. Sauté without colouring it. Drain the rice well and add to pan. Mix through to coat the rice with ghee evenly. Add the same quantity of water as rice. Add some salt and bring to the boil quickly. Stir gently. Simmer at an even temperature until all the water on the surface is absorbed. Cover with a tight-fitting lid and place in a preheated 180°C (350°F/gas 4) oven for 15 minutes or until all the water is absorbed. Remove the pan from the oven and stir through gently without breaking the grains.

While this is a basic 'pulao' recipe, there are several vegetables or meats that can be added to cook with the rice. Depending on the region from which the pulao originates, the ingredients vary slightly. A very popular pulao is made with green peas. Most restaurants tend to add some turmeric to attain an orange colour.

This recipe can be used as a part of a meal. This style is more popular with the North Indian dishes.

kanegach pulao

wild mushroom pilaf

A unique 'pulao' style rice that hails from Kashmir. This recipe uses the technique of cooking rice with a spice mix. The flavours and the aroma, if done well, are magical.

SERVES: 4

3 cups basmati rice

250 g (9 oz) dried wild mushrooms

2 onions

½ cup ghee

pinch saffron

2 cm (³/₄ in.) piece ginger

2 green chillies

1 tsp cumin seeds

1 small cinnamon stick

5 cardamom pods

5 cloves

2 bay leaves

½ tsp ground turmeric

½ cup yoghurt

salt

Wash rice and soak for 30 minutes. Soak the mushrooms in some lukewarm water for the same time. Slice a quarter of the onions evenly and finely. Brown in some ghee, drain and set aside for garnish. Dice remaining onions. Soak saffron in some warm water and set aside. Peel and chop up the ginger. Deseed chillies and chop finely.

Heat remaining ghee and add cumin seeds. Cook until they splutter then add all the other whole spices. Stir gently over a moderate heat until all the flavours are released into the oil. Add chopped onions, sauté well. Add chillies and ginger. Add turmeric, stir well and stir in the mushrooms. Fry well, then reduce heat and add beaten yoghurt. Season with some salt and add rice. Stir gently until the rice is mixed in well. Pour in water to cover the mix by 1 cm (½ in.). Bring to the boil rapidly on a high heat and then reduce to simmer. Stir gently without breaking the grains. When most of the water is absorbed, sprinkle in the saffron with its liquid.

Cover with a tight-fitting lid and place in a preheated 180°C (350°F/ gas 4) oven for nearly 15 minutes or until all the moisture is absorbed. Toss with a fork to remove excess steam and prevent overcooking.

Garnish with the browned onions.

I have tried this recipe with fresh wild mushrooms too and the result is outstanding.

Can be a meal in itself when accompanied by yoghurt, or used as a part of a meal.

daal pulao

rice with yellow lentils

A very typical dish among a section of Karnataka, a southern state.

SERVES: 4

2 cups short-grain rice
1 cup yellow lentils
1 cm (½ in.) piece ginger
2 green chillies
½ cup fresh coconut, grated
1 tsp cumin seeds
80 g (2¾ oz) baby eggplant
1 cup oil
1 tsp mustard seeds
1 sprig fresh curry leaves
½ tsp ground turmeric
salt

Wash and drain the rice and lentils together. Peel and finely chop ginger. Deseed and chop chillies finely. Put chillies, coconut and cumin seeds into a blender and puree (add a little water if needed). Remove the stalk and cut eggplant into long thin wedges.

Heat oil in a pan. Add mustard seeds and then the curry leaves. After they splutter, add the eggplant and turmeric. Stir well and then add the coconut paste and some salt. Add the rice and lentil mix, stir well. Add about 4 cups of water or just enough to cook the rice. Bring to the boil, stirring occasionally. Cover with a tight-fitting lid and cook on lower heat for a further 10 minutes. The mix should cook dry. Serve hot.

Although this recipe suggests eggplants, other vegetables may also be added such as gourd vegetables, beans or carrots.

A good accompaniment to most dishes from the region of Karnataka. Alternatively, if cooked with plenty of vegetables, it could be served as a meal with some yoghurt relish.

navarattan pulao

pilaf with 'nine gems'

A typical North Indian style pilaf, this dish is a treat for vegetarians. There are several renditions of this classical Moghlai style pilaf. I have simplified it and have left some room for the cook's imagination too.

SERVES: 4

2½ cups basmati rice

200 g (7 oz) mixture of carrots, potatoes, long melons (Chinese melons), cauliflower, paneer*, raw cashews, sultanas, beans, peas

pinch saffron

1 onion

½ cup ghee

5 cardamom pods

1 cinnamon stick

4 cloves

2 bay leaves

1 tsp cumin seeds

salt

Wash the rice well, soak for an hour and drain well. Peel and dice carrots, potatoes and long melons into pea-sized cubes. Cut cauliflower into small florets, blanch and refresh. Dice paneer into pieces of the same size and lightly fry, then cool. Soak saffron in some warm water. Slice onion thinly. Sauté the cashews and sultanas in some ghee until cashews are golden brown, drain and set aside. In the same ghee, fry one-third of the finely sliced onion until golden brown and set aside for garnish.

Heat remaining ghee and put in all the whole spices. Stir through to allow them to release their flavours into the ghee. Add remaining sliced onions and sauté gently without colouring. Add some salt and all the vegetables except peas. Sauté well. Add the rice and stir gently, taking care not to break the grains. Add enough water to cover the rice by 1 cm (¹/₂ in.) (generally 1¹/₄ times the volume of rice, depending on the quality of rice). Add the saffron with the water. Bring to the boil quickly and then reduce the heat and simmer. As the water starts getting absorbed into the rice, add the peas.

Cover with a tight-fitting lid and cook on low heat. The whole pot may be put into a preheated 150°C (300°F/gas 2) oven too, if possible. Cook for about 15 minutes and remove the lid. Gently stir up the rice with a fork. Add the paneer, cashews and sultanas and mix through with the fork.

*The recipe for Paneer (Fresh curd cheese) can be found on page 190.

The vegetables can be varied depending on the season or availability.

I use this with the equally aromatic 'Royal' goat shanks (Nizami nalli khorma, see recipe page 93). This rice dish also has the makings of a meal in itself with some 'raita', or yoghurt relish.

zaffrani pulao

saffron pilaf

Probably the best-known rice dish in Indian restaurants outside of India, whether or not saffron is actually added to the pilaf! It is very aromatic and is a fairly simple and quick recipe to prepare.

SERVES: 4

3 cups basmati rice
1 onion
¼ cup ghee
pinch saffron
8 cardamom pods
salt

Wash rice well and soak for an hour. Slice onion and fry half to a golden brown in the ghee. Drain well and cool, reserving the ghee. Soak saffron in some warm water.

Heat reserved ghee in a pan. Add the cardamom pods and sauté until all the flavours are released into the ghee. Add the remaining onion and sauté without colouring. Add the rice and toss gently to prevent the grains from breaking. Add enough water to cover the rice by 1 cm (½ in.). Add the saffron with the water, and some salt. Bring to the boil over a high heat. Stir gently and then reduce the heat to simmer, allowing the rice to absorb the moisture.

Cover with a tight-fitting lid and cook on a low and even heat for a further 15 minutes or in a preheated 150°C (300°F/gas 2) oven for the same time. When the rice is just cooked, gently turn over with a fork to allow the steam to escape.

Some vegetables or meats may be added to this dish, depending on the requirements of the meal. However, I wouldn't recommend anything overpowering that could take away the subtle flavours of cardamom and saffron with the rice.

A common accompaniment to a lot of North Indian dishes.

chole palak pulao

chickpea and spinach pilaf

Although there is a bit more involved than in a plain pilaf, this is a hearty treat and worth the effort.
It is traditionally a special occasion rice dish.

SERVES: 4

½ cup chickpeas

2 cups basmati rice

5 cardamom pods

1 tsp cumin seeds

2 bay leaves

150 g (5½ oz) English spinach

1 onion

3 cloves garlic

½ cup ghee

½ cup yoghurt

salt

1 tsp garam masala*

Wash chickpeas and soak for 4 hours. Wash rice and soak separately for an hour. Drain chickpeas, cover with fresh water in a pot and boil. Add half the cardamom, cumin and a bay leaf to the pot. Simmer until the chickpeas are just cooked, drain and save the liquid. Heat a little water in the pan, add cleaned spinach leaves and cook. Refresh and prepare a fine puree of spinach. Peel onion and garlic and chop very finely.

Heat ghee in a pan. Add the rest of the whole spices and swirl around in the ghee. Add the onion and garlic, sauté well. When the mix turns golden brown, add chickpeas and sauté well. Add beaten yoghurt and cook until all the moisture has evaporated. Then add the rice and toss gently to prevent the grains from breaking. Add enough liquid (from boiling the chickpeas) to cover the rice by 1 cm (½ in.). Add some salt. Bring to the boil then reduce the heat and simmer. When the water is nearly fully absorbed into the rice, add the spinach. Again, mix gently. Sprinkle the garam masala over.

Cover and finish cooking either in a 150°C (300°F/gas 2) oven or on the stove top on a low heat for about 8 minutes or until the rice is fully cooked and the mix dry. Turn the rice over with a fork to release the steam.

Serve immediately.

*The recipe for Garam masala (Aromatic spice mix) can be found on page 190.

The chickpeas may be replaced with some meat if desired.

You can serve this as a meal, accompanied by some yoghurt relish or 'raita'. It can be served as part of a North Indian style meal too.

andhra kodi pulao

spicy chicken pilaf

Distinguished by spicy and coconut flavours, this very traditional chicken pilaf is from
the southern state of Andhra Pradesh.

SERVES: 4

2 cups basmati rice

200 g (7 oz) chicken
   thigh fillets

1 onion

2 cm (³/₄ in.) piece ginger

4 green chillies

2 tbsp tamarind pulp

½ cup oil

1 tsp cumin seeds

1 sprig fresh curry leaves

salt

2 cups coconut cream

Wash and soak the rice. Cut up the chicken into 1.5 cm (²/₃ in.) cubes. Peel and slice onion. Peel ginger and cut into long strips. Slit chillies. Prepare tamarind pulp (see page 9).

Heat oil in a pan, add the cumin seeds and then curry leaves. Add chillies and ginger. Sauté well. Add onion, and sauté until translucent. Add the chicken and some salt. Seal well on high heat. Add the rice and toss gently. Once mixed, add the coconut cream and bring to the boil. Add some water so that the rice and chicken mix is well covered by the cooking liquid. Taste and adjust the seasoning. Simmer over a gentle heat, stirring occasionally.

Cover and cook until all the moisture is absorbed. This could also be done in a preheated 150°C (300°F/gas 2) oven for about 15 minutes. When the rice is fully cooked, open the lid and stir gently.

Traditionally this is a very hot dish, but you can adjust the quantity of chillies to suit your palate.

Serve with some yoghurt relish or 'raita' or as a part of a meal.

chemmeen pulao

spicy prawns with rice

A spicy rice and prawn combination that can be a meal in itself.

SERVES: 4

2 cups basmati rice

2 cups peeled fresh prawns

1 onion

2 tomatoes

3 green chillies

2.5 cm (1 in.) piece ginger

6 cloves garlic

3 tbsp oil

1 tsp ghee

4 cardamom pods

2 bay leaves

1 tsp black peppercorns

¼ tsp ground turmeric

salt

½ cup coconut cream

2 sprigs fresh coriander

Wash rice well and drain. Wash prawn meat well. Peel onion and tomatoes and chop finely. Deseed chillies and peel ginger and garlic. Put chillies, ginger and garlic in a blender and prepare a smooth paste.

Heat the oil and ghee together in a pan. Add cardamom, bay leaves and peppercorns and cook until they crackle. Add the onions and sauté well, then add turmeric and chilli puree. Cook well, stirring, and add the chopped tomatoes and some salt. Stir until the mix cooks into a thick paste.

Add prawns and seal them, then add the rice. Add the coconut cream and two cups of water. Adjust the seasoning and stir. Bring back to the boil quickly. Reduce the heat and simmer until most of the moisture has been absorbed by the rice. Add some more water if required to cook the rice. Cover with a tight-fitting lid and cook on a very low heat for a further 10 minutes. When the rice is fully cooked, toss gently with a fork, without breaking the rice grains. Serve hot, garnished with chopped coriander.

Most shellfish would work well in place of the prawns. Cooking times may vary accordingly.

DESSERTS

After all the spices and heady aromas of an Indian meal, it is almost essential to indulge in something sweet to finish off. But desserts are not just a course in a meal, they have a much broader place in the culture. They are an essential part of living for all classes of people, and are made as offerings in temples for any religious festival and given as gifts for auspicious occasions, festivals or even significant days such as birthdays and anniversaries. There are specific desserts that are made for particular festivals.

As with all the other recipes, desserts vary from region to region. Some regions are better known for sweets than others (for example, Bengal is famous for a number of sweets that have become popular throughout the world), but there are some gems in each and every corner of India. Some sweets, such as rice pudding, are found all over India and yet the recipe varies completely from region to region.

Indian desserts can generally be classified into milk based, sugar based or fruit (or vegetable) based, although some unique ones would be difficult to categorise under any of those headings. The basic flavourings used in most recipes are cardamom, saffron, vetiver (essence), kewra (screwpine flower essence) and rose syrup. One unique thing with some Indian desserts is the use of 'varq', a very finely beaten silver leaf. Some use gold leaf too—and yes, it is edible gold and silver in pure form!

Like pastry chefs, Indian sweet makers or 'halwais' are considered to be specialists who require skill and artistry. But apart from the fact that the measurements in the recipes have to be accurate and precise, I believe that the similarity ends there. Indian sweets can be produced by anyone once some basic steps are mastered. I have selected a few desserts that are traditional, or based on a traditional recipe but with my own twist. You can feel free to be creative too.

shrikhand

sweetened yoghurt

A simple dessert that hails from Western India. This is really a great summer sweet.

SERVES: 4

4 cups yoghurt
2 tbsp milk
pinch saffron
1 tsp cardamom seeds
1½ cups caster sugar
1 tbsp pistachios
1 tbsp sunflower seeds

Put the yoghurt into a muslin cloth, tie up and hang, so as to drain out all the whey. Warm the milk and soak the saffron strand in it. Dry-roast and crush the cardamom seeds.

Put the yoghurt into a bowl and add the sugar. Mix and rest for a few minutes to allow the sugar to melt into the yoghurt. Add the saffron and milk and the ground cardamom and whisk well, using a blender if available, until all the ingredients are mixed and yoghurt is light and creamy. Taste for sweetness; add more sugar if desired. Garnish with the pistachios and sunflower seeds.

There are many ways to flavour the shrikhand. One of the more popular flavours in India is mango, when in season. However, over the years I have used different stone fruits and summer berries effectively.

Lovely when served with the Cardamom and ginger biscuit (Adrak aur elaichi ka biskut, see recipe page 161) and seasonal berries.

adrak aur elaichi ka biskut

cardamom and ginger biscuit

A good snack with coffee, this biscuit can also be used with a dessert to add a crisp texture.
Shape and cook them according to the intended use.

SERVES: 4

4 egg whites
1 cup caster sugar
1 cup plain flour
¼ cup fine semolina
½ cup unsalted butter
½ tsp cardamom seeds
½ tsp ground ginger
1 tbsp pistachios, peeled

In a mixing bowl, whisk egg whites and slowly add sugar. Gently stir flour and semolina into mixture and then fold in melted butter. Crush cardamom seeds and add, along with the ginger. Mix and refrigerate for 15 minutes or until required. Chop up pistachios finely.

Divide the dough into 8 equal portions. Roll into balls and flatten in the palms of your hands. Place on a baking tray. Sprinkle with pistachios. Bake in a preheated 180°C (350°F/gas 4) oven for 5 minutes. The mix will spread out a bit and get a golden brown finish. If a crisper finish is desired, reduce the temperature and extend the cooking time.

I have experimented with several different spices and flavourings for this recipe. A small amount of crushed pepper instead of ginger gives a great result, especially when served with a very sweet dessert.

I have used this recipe (without the semolina) and spread the mix to form a crispy biscuit to serve with other desserts. You could shape the biscuit over an inverted cup to make a pastry cup in which to present a dessert such as Shrikhand (Sweetened yoghurt, see recipe page 160). Alternatively, spread the mix into thin strips, mould after cooking while still hot, or spread evenly on a large baking tray and cut into desired shapes and then mould (geometrically or with cookie cutters) while still hot and use as garnish.

bebinca

goan layered pudding

I rate this as one of the kings of confections—not just from Goa, but from the whole country. Preparation is time consuming and labour intensive, but it is worth the effort. I have simplified it as far as possible from the very traditional method where the coconut milk is extracted manually.

SERVES: 4

4 eggs

1 cup sugar

1½ tins (500 ml/16 fl oz) coconut cream

1 cup plain flour

½ nutmeg

½ cup unsalted clarified butter

In a mixing bowl, whisk eggs well and slowly add sugar. Blend well until all the sugar dissolves. Add the coconut cream and continue to whisk. Gently stir flour into mixture and whisk well to ensure there are no lumps. Add grated nutmeg. An electric beater may be used to prepare the batter if available. The final batter should be of pouring consistency, similar to a pancake batter.

Brush a loaf tin with melted clarified butter. Pour a ladleful of the batter into the tin, spread well and cook under the grill until the surface is golden brown. Brush with clarified butter and repeat the process until all the batter is used up. Ideally, this dessert should have 15–17 layers. When the last layer is cooked, cover the tin with foil and bake in a preheated 170°C (325°F/gas 3) oven for 10 minutes. Cool and demould. Slice and serve at room temperature.

Depending on the occasion, this can be prepared in a ring mould, cake tin, large rectangular tray or, as on our menu, in a loaf tin.

I like to serve this with some fresh mango coulis, treacle and nuts.

paneer ka meetha

sweet curd cheese

I have often experimented with desserts to lighten their sweetness and richness, because some Indian desserts can be quite heavy. Hence this is a non-traditional recipe.

SERVES: 4

400 g (14 oz) paneer*
120 g (4¼ oz) stawberries
5 sprigs fresh mint
small pinch fennel seeds
1 tbsp sliced almonds
1½ tbsp cornflour
2 cups full cream milk
1½ cups condensed milk
½ cup sugar (optional)

Prepare paneer but do not shape it. When fully drained, turn out into a bowl and break up with a ladle. Slice some strawberries for garnish and dice the rest. Pick the mint leaves, puree and extract juice by squeezing through muslin cloth. Dry-roast fennel and grind to a powder with a mortar and pestle. Toast the almonds lightly.

Dissolve the cornflour in a little cold milk. Heat the remaining milk in a pan and reduce to almost half its volume. Remove from heat, add condensed milk, fennel powder and stir in the cornflour mix. Return to the heat and bring to the boil, stirring. Pour the mix over the paneer and mix well. Mix in the diced strawberries. Taste and adjust the sweetness by adding some sugar, if desired. Place into dariole moulds. Refrigerate to set well.

The sugar in this recipe is optional for making sugar shards to use as a garnish. To prepare sugar shards, sprinkle sugar on a greased baking tray and bake in a 180°C (350°F/gas 4) oven until the sugar is caramelised into a thin sheet. Remove, cool and lift off the sugar into large uneven-shaped shards.

Serve chilled, garnished with sliced strawberries, almonds and sugar shards, and sprinkled with mint juice.

*The recipe for Paneer (Fresh curd cheese) can be found on page 190.

Try this recipe with a combination of fruits. I have served this with kiwifruit and strawberries, which have worked well due to the contrast in tastes. The sugar for garnish can be varied to any other creative form of sugar—be it pulled, strung or formed into a net.

pineapple sheera

semolina pudding with pineapple

Several desserts such as this are made in many different regions of India. The styles vary depending on the region the dessert comes from. This version from the western state of Maharashtra is called 'sheera'.

SERVES: 4

pinch saffron
100 g (3½ oz) pineapple
½ tsp cardamom seeds
1 tbsp cashews
1 tbsp sultanas
1½ tbsp ghee
2 cups semolina
½ cup sugar

Soak saffron in some warm water. Chop pineapple into small cubes. Dry-roast cardamom seeds and crush to a powder. Sauté cashews and sultanas in some ghee, drain and cool.

Heat remaining ghee in a pan. Add semolina and stir well. Continue to cook until semolina is nicely roasted. Add sugar, pineapple and cardamom. Stir well. Add the cashews and sultanas. Add 300 ml (10 fl oz) boiling water and stir well. Add the saffron and its liquid. Stir well until the semolina starts leaving the sides of the pan. Serve hot or at room temperature.

Experiment with different fruits other than pineapple.

anjeer aur akhrot ki kulfi

frozen parfait with figs and walnuts

Kulfi is traditionally a frozen sweet, much like an ice-cream, except that the base is milk which is reduced over low heat for hours to obtain a condensed form called 'rabri'. Considering the time demands of the process, I have used some condensed milk to make things simple.

SERVES: 4

2 tbsp dried figs
2 tbsp walnuts
1 tbsp pistachios
4 cardamom pods
1 cup milk
1 cup cream
2 cups condensed milk
1 tbsp rose syrup

Chop up the figs and walnuts into small pieces. Slice pistachios. Peel and crush the cardamom.

Mix milk and cream in a pan. Add crushed cardamom. Bring to the boil and simmer, stirring continuously. Reduce the mix to nearly half its volume. Add the condensed milk and stir. Add the figs and walnuts (save some for garnish) and remove from the heat. Chill completely for 3 hours in the fridge and churn in an ice-cream machine. When the mix starts to set in the machine, scoop out into kulfi moulds, or any ramekin or dariole moulds if that is more convenient. Freeze for 4 hours or until well set. Kulfi can be presented whole or cut and served garnished with the rose syrup and the reserved figs and nuts.

If an ice-cream machine is not available, reduce the quantity of milk to 2$^1/_2$ tablespoons and increase the quantity of cream to 1$^1/_2$ cups. Follow the same process as above. After chilling, pour directly into moulds and freeze until well set.

semiyaa payasam

vermicelli pudding

Vermicelli pudding is made in several regions of India. It varies from being as dry as an Asian stir-fried noodle dish to having a thin soup-like consistency, depending on the region. Some serve it hot, others cold, set in a mud pot! This is a very versatile dessert and I have picked one of my favourite versions, from the southern state of Kerala.

SERVES: 4

1 tbsp ghee
1 tbsp raw cashews
1 tbsp sultanas
250 g (9 oz) vermicelli
4 cups milk
½ cup sugar
½ tsp cardamom seeds

Heat ghee in a pan and gently sauté the cashews and sultanas. Remove cashews and sultanas and return ghee to the heat. Break up vermicelli into small pieces and toss in the ghee on gentle heat until golden brown, then drain. Heat milk and sugar in a pan and bring to the boil. Stir and cook until all the sugar is dissolved and milk is reduced by at least one-quarter. Dry-roast cardamom and grind to a powder.

Bring the reduced milk to the boil, add the vermicelli and simmer. Cook for a couple of minutes. Add the nuts, sultanas and the ground cardamom. Simmer until cooked. Remove from the heat.

May be served hot, at room temperature or chilled.

patishapta

pancakes with coconut

A truly unique dessert from Bengal. These pancakes are filled with fresh coconut and sugar
and are quite simple to prepare.

SERVES: 4

120 g (4¼ oz) semolina

350 ml (12 fl oz) milk

225 g (8 oz) plain flour

85 g (3 oz) sugar

200 g (7 oz) fresh coconut, grated

120 g (4¼ oz) full cream
    milk powder

½ tsp ground cardamom

1 tbsp oil

To make the batter, soak semolina in milk for about an hour. Stir well. Add the sifted plain flour and 3 tablespoons of sugar and whisk to avoid forming any lumps. To make the filling, mix remaining sugar with coconut in a pan and cook gently until the sugar dissolves and the mix becomes sticky. Take pan off the heat and add the milk powder and cardamom. Add a spoonful of water to homogenise the mix. Put back on the heat and gently stir until the mix is cooked. Remove and cool.

Heat a non-stick pan. Spoon in 2 ladles of the batter and swirl around the pan. Cook the pancake over medium heat, without browning. Turn over and cook the other side of the pancake, again without browning. Spoon in a little oil if the batter sticks. Remove to a plate or a clean kitchen bench. Spoon one-eighth of the filling into the pancake and spread. Roll pancake up like a Swiss roll. Repeat the process until all 8 pancakes are made and the filling is used up.

This recipe is truly the traditional way of making these pancakes except for the use of milk powder. I have used milk powder only because 'khoa', or solidified milk, which is traditionally used, may not be readily available. You can experiment with different fillings. I have tried strawberries with the coconut and sugar with a very good result, because the sourness of strawberry cuts the sweetness.

Traditionally, these may be served hot or cold and the accompaniment is 'rabri', or condensed fresh milk.

khajoor bhara malpoa

date-filled pancakes

Traditionally, 'malpoa' is a pancake that is fried and soaked in thick sugar syrup and served with 'rabri'
(the reduced milk explained on page 166). However, we have altered the recipe slightly and incorporated a filling,
and found the result to be stunning.

SERVES: 4

1½ cups fresh dates
½ cup cream
1 cup sugar
pinch saffron
1 cinnamon stick
1 L (35 fl oz) milk
50 g (1¾ oz) fine semolina
50 g (1¾ oz) plain flour
1 tbsp ghee
1 tsp raw pistachios

Slit dates and remove the seeds. Saving 4 dates for garnish, chop up the rest into small pieces. Warm cream with a spoonful of sugar and the saffron; simmer for a few minutes and set aside. Heat remaining sugar with 1 tablespoon of water and the cinnamon and cook to a syrupy consistency. Add the chopped dates and cook for a few minutes until all the moisture is absorbed. Break the dates up to almost a mash. Remove cinnamon and cool.

Heat the milk and simmer until reduced to nearly half the volume. Add semolina and flour to the milk and whisk to obtain a lump-free batter of pouring consistency. The consistency of the batter is really important in getting the pancake right. While the quantities given above have been tried and tested, the consistency depends on the fineness of the semolina, the strength of the flour, etc. So adjust the consistency with some milk if need be to obtain a smooth pancake batter.

Heat a non-stick pan. Spoon some ghee into the pan. Spoon one-quarter of the batter into the pan and spread evenly by swirling around. Cook over moderate heat, turn over and complete cooking. Spoon a little ghee around the pancake. Turn out the pancake when done onto a flat surface, spread the date mix on it and roll tightly. Set aside. Slice as desired and serve with the saffron cream, chopped pistachios and the halved dates for garnish.

Traditionally, these pancakes are made with exactly the same recipe, but without any filling. When completely fried they are soaked in the sugar syrup and then served with the cream. It is certainly rich and a special occasion dessert. I have lightened it by reducing the ghee and sugar.

Beaten silver leaf or gold leaf, when available, would lend itself very well to this dessert.

saeb ka samosa

apple in pastry triangles

Here's a rule bender. Samosas are a very well known traditional snack. I have created this recipe on the same principle except it has a sweet filling as opposed to savoury.

SERVES: 4

PASTRY

3 cups plain flour
½ tsp sugar
1 tsp ground cardamom
salt
1 cup unsalted butter

FILLING

1 kg (2 lb 4 oz) cooking apples
2 cups sugar
1 cinnamon stick
½ cup almond meal
½ cup sultanas
1 sprig fresh mint

oil to deep-fry

TO PREPARE THE PASTRY: Sift the flour into a bowl. Add sugar, cardamom and a pinch of salt. Rub the butter into the flour gently. Add enough water to form a stiff dough. Cover with a damp cloth and set aside while preparing filling. Once filling is cooling, divide the dough into 6 equal parts and roll into balls. Dust with a little flour and roll out into long, thin strips roughly 4 mm (¹/₆ in.) thick, 15 cm (6 in.) long and 6 cm (2¹/₂ in.) wide. Set aside in the fridge for 15 minutes.

TO PREPARE THE FILLING: Peel, core and roughly dice apples into 1 cm (¹/₂ in.) pieces. Put the sugar, apples, cinnamon stick and 1 tablespoon of water in a pan. Cook the apples, stirring occasionally, until all the moisture is absorbed. Add the almond meal and sultanas, saving a few for garnish, and mix well. Remove from the heat. Add finely chopped mint leaves. Refrigerate the mix.

TO ASSEMBLE: Get the pastry strips, the filling, a pastry brush and some water. Cut the strips in half along the width, giving 12 small pastry pieces. Take one strip in the palm of your left hand; holding the straight cut side along the index finger. Brush along the perimeter with a little water. Fold the dough inwards from both ends, overlapping each other, similar to preparing a paper piping bag. Press the tip (which should be at the centre of the straight cut side) and along the sides to seal. Cup the cone-shaped pastry shell in your palm, keeping the opening side up. Spoon one-twelfth of the filling into this cavity. Brush water around the opening and fold over the back of the cone to seal with the front. Seal well; tidy the edges up by cutting off the extra pastry. Press down the base with a fork if necessary, or crimp. Refrigerate for a few minutes before cooking. When ready, deep-fry over medium heat until the pastry is golden brown.

Serve the samosas hot with a scoop of good vanilla bean ice cream and some rose syrup.

shahi paarche

bread pudding

I do get a reaction of disbelief from some customers when we feature this dessert on the menu at Qmin. Bread pudding on an Indian menu? Yes, the Nizams of Hyderabad enjoyed this bread pudding a century ago. Truly a sensational dish.

SERVES: 4

1 tbsp blanched pistachios

1 tbsp blanched whole almonds

8 slices white bread

1 cup ghee

2 eggs

1 tbsp sugar

½ cup cream

pinch saffron

½ tsp mix of ground mace and
   ground cardamom

Soak the pistachios and almonds (saving some of each for garnish) in some warm water for an hour or so to soften. Cut bread slices into desired shape. Heat ghee in a pan. Fry the bread slices and drain well, reserving ghee for later use. Put pistachios and almonds in a blender and puree. Transfer to a mixing bowl, add eggs, sugar and cream and whisk until light. Soak saffron in some warm water. Warm the reserved ghee in the pan and stir in the mace, cardamom and saffron. Pour spice mix into the egg mix, whisking well.

Arrange the bread slices in a greased ovenproof dish. Pour the egg mix over. Bake in a preheated 180°C (350°F/gas 4) oven for about 20 minutes, until a light golden brown crust is formed. Serve hot, garnished with reserved nuts.

The shape that you cut the bread into depends on how it will be served—as individual portions or baked in a big dish.

Traditionally, this is garnished with nuts and a beaten silver leaf called 'varak'. I also use some double cream and berries to add to the presentation.

kaddu ka halwa

pumpkin pudding

Although I have called this a 'pudding', it is unlike a traditional steamed or baked pudding.

SERVES: 4

1 small 700–800 g (1½ lb)
   butternut pumpkin
2 tbsp unsalted cashews
2 tbsp raisins
3 tbsp ghee
1 cup sugar
1½ cups milk
1 tbsp honey
½ tsp ground cardamom

Peel, deseed and grate pumpkin. Squeeze out pumpkin to remove all the moisture. Fry the cashews and raisins in ghee in a heavy-based pan on low heat until golden brown. Add the grated pumpkin and fry gently. Add sugar and cook, stirring, for 3–4 minutes. Then add milk and honey; cook until mixture is soft and dry, stirring occasionally. Add cardamom to finish off and serve hot.

The pudding presents well when moulded in dariole moulds or as quenelles.

I have used butternut pumpkin for this recipe, but it can be varied by using another type of pumpkin or, alternatively, white long squash or gourd.

ACCOMPANIMENTS

Although this chapter is right at the end of the book, it is one of the most important. Those who have experienced an Indian meal from any region would have noticed that no meal is complete without the pickles, chutneys, sauces and dips.

Because of the weather conditions and lack of refrigeration in ancient days, preserving food is a traditional method of extending the use of foodstuffs. There are regions where even meat is pickled, heavily doused in spices and completely dehydrated to prevent spoilage. However, all the recipes here are preservative-free and should be prepared freshly for consumption. The list of chutneys, relishes and spices is almost endless, so I've limited myself here to specific items that would make good accompaniments to other recipes in this book.

One dish that couldn't be left out is 'daal' or lentils. 'Daal–roti' is the staple diet almost everywhere, and there are numerous varieties of legumes available and hundreds of different dishes. They can range from a thin watery soup, to thick as white sauce, to completely dry like soft grains. I have listed two of the most popular recipes.

I have given recipes for three distinctly different gravies that are extremely useful in preparing an Indian meal. 'Makhni' is by far the most popular as it's the base of 'Butter chicken', which has a million renditions around the globe. The other two gravies are good for preparing a generic Indian style stew. I have also added the recipe for 'paneer', a fresh curd cheese which is very versatile in Indian cooking.

There are as many recipes for 'garam masala' (literally hot spice mix) as there are cooks, and they can include anything from cumin to dried rose petals! Here is one variation.

Although I have recommended the use of each of these recipes with specific items, feel free to use them as you please. For example, the Pineapple chutney adds zing to a nicely roasted pork loin, or try Garlic chutney with some toasted sourdough bread.

brinjal gojju

eggplant chutney

8 baby eggplants

salt

8 shallots

5 green chillies

3 tbsp tamarind pulp

2 tbsp oil

1 tsp brown mustard seeds

¼ tsp ground turmeric

Remove the stalks and dice the eggplants into even 1.5 cm (²/₃ in.) cubes. Sprinkle with some salt and set aside for 20 minutes. Wash off salt and soak eggplants in water. Peel shallots and finely dice. Chop up the chillies finely. Prepare tamarind pulp (see page 9).

Heat oil in a pan. Add the mustard seeds and cook until they crackle, then add the shallots and turmeric. Sauté without colouring. Add the chillies and sauté well, without browning. Drain eggplants well and add to pan. Continue to stir-fry. Check and adjust the seasoning. When the eggplant is cooked well, add the tamarind pulp. Simmer until the mix cooks to a thick, chutney-like consistency. Cool and place in a clean jar.

pudhina chutney

mint chutney

2 bunches fresh spearmint

1 bunch fresh coriander

5 green chillies

2 cm (³/₄ in.) piece ginger

salt

½ cup yoghurt

    or 2 tbsp tamarind pulp

Pick and wash the mint and coriander leaves. Slit the chillies, remove the seeds and chop. Peel the ginger and chop up. Grind all these ingredients together in a blender to form a paste. Add some salt and set aside. This mix may be preserved by adding a thin layer of oil on top and storing in the refrigerator.

When ready to serve, add beaten yoghurt or tamarind pulp (see page 9) and mix well. Adjust seasoning and serve cold.

pineapple gojju

pineapple chutney

4 shallots

2 tomatoes

2 green chillies

500 g (1 lb 2 oz) pineapple

1½ tbsp tamarind pulp

½ cup oil

½ tsp brown mustard seeds

1 sprig fresh curry leaves

2 dried red chillies

½ tsp ground turmeric

salt

Peel shallots and chop finely. Blanch tomatoes and chop up finely. Deseed the green chillies and chop up. Dice the pineapple into small cubes. Prepare tamarind pulp (see page 9).

Heat oil in a pan. Add mustard seeds, cook until they crackle, then add the curry leaves and broken dried red chillies. Add shallots and sauté well without colouring. Add green chillies and turmeric. Add tomatoes and a pinch of salt. Cook until the oil almost separates from the mix. Add the pineapple and stir. Simmer, stirring occasionally, and reduce until most of the moisture evaporates from the pineapple. Add the tamarind pulp and continue to reduce. Taste and adjust the seasoning. When chutney consistency is reached, remove from the heat and cool.

If you like, add some asafoetida with the curry leaves and/or some garlic with the chillies.

nalikera chutney

fresh coconut chutney

3 red chillies

1 onion

2 cups fresh coconut, grated

1 green chilli (optional)

2 tbsp yoghurt

1 tsp roasted split chickpeas

pinch sugar

salt

½ cup oil

½ tsp black mustard seeds

1 sprig fresh curry leaves

Split 2 red chillies, fry and remove from pan. Chop and sauté onion. Mix onion, coconut, green chilli (if used), fried chillies, yoghurt, chickpeas, sugar and some salt. Grind in a blender until smooth. Heat oil in a pan and add remaining chilli, the mustard seeds and curry leaves; pour over the blended mix. Mix through with a spoon and serve.

lasanachi chutney

garlic chutney

1 cup fresh coconut, grated

1 tsp white sesame seeds

1 tsp tamarind pulp

4 cloves garlic

½ tsp chilli powder

pinch sugar

salt

Dry-roast the coconut in a pan over medium heat until light brown, stirring continuously. Set aside. Dry-roast the sesame seeds and add to the coconut. Prepare the tamarind pulp (see page 9). Peel the garlic and mix in with all the other ingredients. Crush using a mortar and pestle until a uniform dry mix is obtained.

If unavailable, fresh coconut may be replaced with desiccated.

tamatar ka kut

tomato relish

500 g (1 lb 2 oz) cherry
   tomatoes
2 tbsp oil
1 sprig fresh curry leaves
1 tsp cumin seeds
1 tsp fennel seeds
1 tsp nigella seeds
1 tsp fenugreek seeds
1 tsp brown mustard seeds
2 cm (¾ in.) piece ginger
½ tsp chilli powder
½ tsp sugar
salt

Blanch cherry tomatoes and cut into quarters. Heat oil in a pan. Add the curry leaves and then the whole spices. When sautéed, add chopped ginger, chilli powder, then tomatoes, sugar and some salt. Mix well, simmer for a few minutes.

Traditionally, medium-sized tomatoes are used with the skin on. I find cherry tomatoes more suited to this recipe.

kichadi

cucumber and yoghurt relish

2 Lebanese cucumbers
salt
1 tsp mustard seeds
2 green chillies
½ cup fresh coconut, grated
½ cup yoghurt
2 tbsp oil
2 dried red chillies
few fresh curry leaves

Peel cucumber and dice into small cubes. Sprinkle with some salt and set aside for half an hour. Put half the mustard seeds, the chopped green chillies and the coconut into a blender and grind into a paste. Add a spoonful of yoghurt if required to aid blending. Squeeze the cucumbers to remove all the liquid. Whip yoghurt. Mix with cucumber and add the blended coconut mix. Heat the oil in a small pan. Add the remaining mustard seeds, the red chillies, broken in half, and curry leaves. When cooked, pour over the cucumber mix and stir in. Adjust the seasoning.

dahi palak

yoghurt and spinach relish

2 cups yoghurt
½ tsp sugar
salt
1 green chilli
2 tbsp oil
1 tsp cumin seeds
250 g (9 oz) English spinach
   (baby spinach preferable)

Whisk the yoghurt with sugar and some salt, and set aside in the refrigerator. Deseed the chilli and chop. Heat oil in a pan. Add cumin seeds and then the chilli. Add the spinach leaves (shred the leaves if they are large or leave whole if baby leaves are used). Pour the mix into the yoghurt and mix well. Serve immediately.

kaddu ka raita

pumpkin and yoghurt relish

250 g (9 oz) butternut pumpkin
1 tsp cumin seeds
2 cups yoghurt
¼ tsp chilli powder
1 tsp sugar
salt
2 sprigs fresh coriander

Peel pumpkin and dice into small cubes and steam until cooked. Dry-roast and crush cumin seeds. Whisk the yoghurt with ground cumin, chilli powder, sugar and some salt. Add chopped coriander and the pumpkin and mix gently. Serve chilled.

balchao

pickled prawn relish

GOAN SPICE MIX

1 cup chilli powder

2 tbsp cumin seeds

1 tbsp ground white pepper

1½ tbsp sugar

2 tbsp paprika

1 tbsp smoked paprika

2 tsp ground cloves

2 tbsp garlic powder

1½ cups malt vinegar

salt

½ cup oil

BALCHAO

800 g (1 lb 12 oz) small prawns

salt

½ tsp ground turmeric

1½ onions

2 cm (³/₄ in.) piece ginger

4 cloves garlic

1 cup oil

1 sprig fresh curry leaves

½ cup Goan spice mix

1 tbsp sugar

TO PREPARE THE GOAN SPICE MIX: Mix all Goan spice mix ingredients well in a bowl. Refrigerate.

TO PREPARE THE BALCHAO: Peel prawns, remove heads and tails. Wash the prawn meat and drain well. Rub with salt and turmeric and set aside for about an hour. Drain all the water and juices. Peel onions and dice finely. Peel ginger and garlic and grind into a fine paste. Heat half the oil in a heavy pan. Add the onions, sauté well until light brown. Add the prawns and cook well. Remove from the pan and set aside. Heat the remaining oil; add curry leaves and the ginger and garlic paste. Fry well and add the spice mix. Cook gently on a low heat and reduce, stirring occasionally. Add the prawn mix and sugar. Simmer for another couple of minutes until dry and remove from heat.

Cool and bottle. Take care not to add any water or moisture, so as to preserve for a long period.

The spice mix used in this recipe is truly versatile. This mix by itself, if handled carefully, can be preserved for a long time. It has a typical Goan flavour and can be used in other recipes too. For example, it can be smeared on a topside of beef to marinate before roasting, or cooked with some onions and diced meat like pork for a stew. The traditional method is to use fresh ingredients, soak in malt vinegar and stone grind. This method is labour intensive and time consuming. So I have prepared this recipe with dried ingredients that can be easily prepared in a coffee grinder or blender and mixed with vinegar.

makhni

butter sauce

10 tomatoes
½ tsp chilli powder
salt
½ tsp honey
¼ tsp ground white pepper
½ tsp ground fenugreek
1 cup butter
½ cup cream

Cut tomatoes into chunks. Put in a pan and cook with chilli powder and a pinch of salt. Stir occasionally. When the tomatoes are well cooked, remove from pan, puree and strain through a fine sieve. Return to the pan and simmer until reduced and the sauce starts to thicken. Add the honey, pepper and fenugreek. Cut the butter into pieces. Drop into the sauce and whisk through. Finish off with the cream.

This is the authentic sauce traditionally used for the well-known 'Butter chicken'. Select ripe firm tomatoes with good colour for this sauce.

parsi sauce

tomato sauce

3 beetroots
8 tomatoes
4 cloves garlic
2 tsp chilli powder
1 tbsp sugar
salt
juice of 1 lemon
½ cup tomato ketchup

Peel the beetroot and cut into chunks. Cut tomatoes into chunks. Peel garlic. In a pan, boil beetroot, tomatoes, garlic and chilli powder with sugar and some salt in 1 cup of water. Simmer until the vegetables are well cooked and breaking up. Finish off with the lemon juice and ketchup. Pass through a fine sieve. Return to the pan and bring back to the boil. Cool and store in bottles or jars.

basic gravy 1
tomato-based gravy

5 onions

1½ cups ghee

2 tbsp raw cashews

2 bay leaves

5 cardamom pods

3 cm (1¼ in.) piece ginger

5 cloves garlic

10 tomatoes

1 tsp cumin seeds

1 cinnamon stick

5 cloves

1½ tsp chilli powder

1½ tsp ground coriander

½ tsp ground turmeric

salt

2 tsp garam masala*

Peel onions and slice 1 into even, fine slices. Heat ghee and cook onion slices, stirring well, to obtain an even golden colour. Drain onion and set aside, reserving ghee in the pan. When onion is cool, puree or crush. Cut the rest of the onions into large pieces. Put them into another pan with 1 cup of water, broken cashews, 1 bay leaf and 1 cardamom pod, and bring to the boil. Simmer until onions are cooked and almost broken up. Remove the bay leaf and cardamom pod and make a fine puree of the onions and cashews. Peel ginger and garlic, and puree. Peel and chop up the tomatoes.

Put the first pan back on the heat. Add all the whole spices and sauté. Add the ginger and garlic puree and cook well. Add the ground spices and stir for a couple of minutes. Now add the onion and cashew puree, simmer and reduce until the ghee starts separating. Add tomatoes and adjust the seasoning. Simmer until tomatoes blend into the sauce. Add the crushed browned onions. Simmer and finish off with garam masala.

*The recipe for Garam Masala (Aromatic spice mix) can be found on page 190.

This gravy can be used with meat, chicken or some vegetables. It can be cooked in advance and stored in the fridge or freezer to be used later.

basic gravy 2

khorma-style gravy

5 onions

1 bay leaf

1 cup raw cashews

1 cup yoghurt

3 cm (1¼ in.) piece ginger

6 cloves garlic

1 cup ghee

5 cardamom pods

5 cloves

salt

1 tsp ground white pepper

¼ cup cream

1 tsp ground mace

Peel the onions and cut into large chunks. Put in a pan with the bay leaf and 1¹/₂ cups of water. Bring to the boil, then simmer until the onions are well cooked. Remove the bay leaf and puree onions into a fine liquid. Return to pan and reduce until it thickens slightly. Soak cashews in warm water and set aside for a while to soften. Puree into a fine paste. Whisk the yoghurt to obtain a smooth consistency. Peel ginger and garlic and grind together into a paste.

In a separate pan, heat ghee. Add the cardamom and cloves. Add the ginger and garlic paste. Fry well, add the onion paste and cook on gentle heat, stirring regularly, until the ghee starts separating. Add the cashew paste and stir continuously (cashews tend to stick to the bottom of the pan easily). Reduce the heat and whisk in the yoghurt. Add salt and pepper, stirring continuously for 3–4 minutes. Finish off by whisking in the cream and sprinkle with mace.

mah di daal makhni

black lentils with kidney beans

2½ cups whole black lentils

½ cup red kidney beans

1 tbsp chilli powder

3 cm (1¼ in.) piece ginger

4 cloves garlic

5 cardamom pods

2 cinnamon sticks

5 cloves

2 tomatoes

salt

½ cup cream

1 cup unsalted butter

Wash the lentils and kidney beans and soak together for at least 4 hours or if possible overnight. Drain and put into a pan. Add water—at least 1 ½ times the volume of lentils and beans. Mix in the chilli powder. Crush the ginger and garlic, mix with the whole spices and tie up in a muslin cloth as a bouquet garni. Put this in with the lentils then bring to the boil. Simmer on low heat until the lentils are cooked. Depending on the volume and temperature, this could take over an hour. Stir occasionally. Top up the water if necessary to a level that allows the lentils to turn over in the water.

Cut up the tomatoes and puree in a blender. When the lentils are cooked, add the tomato puree. Simmer for another 15–20 minutes. Remove the muslin parcel. Add a pinch of salt, cream and butter. Whisk well and adjust the seasoning. The daal should have a thick soup-like consistency.

In this North Indian style daal, the butter used is traditionally fresh butter churned at home. A lot of people use large black cardamom pods in the bouquet garni too, as it adds a very earthy aroma to the daal; so try it if it is available.

masaledaar tadka daal

spiced yellow lentils

2 cups yellow lentils
2 green chillies
½ tsp ground turmeric
1 onion
1 tomato
2 dried red chillies
3 sprigs fresh coriander
1 cm (½ in.) piece ginger
2 tbsp ghee
1 tsp cumin seeds
1 tsp brown mustard seeds
salt

Wash lentils thoroughly and place in a pan. Slit the green chillies and add to the lentils. Add twice the amount of water as lentils and bring to the boil. Reduce heat to a simmer and skim off any scum that rises. Add turmeric and stir occasionally. Keep simmering and skimming until the lentils are well cooked and mashed.

Slice onion, cut tomato into quarters, break the dried red chillies in half, chop the coriander, peel the ginger and chop finely. Heat ghee in a small pan. Add the cumin seeds, mustard seeds and then the dried chilli. As these splutter, add the onion. Sauté until well cooked, but without colouring. Add ginger and then tomato. Stir well and pour over the lentils. Add a pinch of salt and stir well. Finish off with chopped coriander leaves.

garam masala

aromatic spice mix

30 g (1 oz) cardamom pods
2 cinnamon sticks
20 g (3/4 oz) cloves
5 bay leaves
15 g (1/2 oz) whole mace
2 nutmegs
30 g (1 oz) black peppercorns
200 g (7 oz) cumin seeds
50 g (1 3/4 oz) coriander seeds

Spread the spices in a roasting pan and dry in a 120°C (235°F/gas 1/2) oven for approximately 20 minutes. Store in a dry, airtight jar. Pound or grind in a coffee grinder and pass through a fine sieve as and when required.

It is best to pound or grind as required, as opposed to the common practice of storing the powdered mix to prevent the mix from losing its aromatic flavours.

paneer

fresh curd cheese

8 cups full cream milk
1 cup cream
1 cup white vinegar
juice of 1 lemon

Bring milk to the boil in a pan, stirring occasionally. Add cream as the milk begins to rise. Add the vinegar and lemon juice. Turn the heat off and stir. The milk will curdle. Drain the whey by straining through a fine muslin cloth and hanging the muslin up for 2 hours. The solids left in the cloth is paneer. Depending on its use, it may be pressed or left creamy. If pressed in muslin under some weight for a few hours, the paneer becomes hardened. It can be shaped into any desired shape. Remove from muslin and chill before cutting.

a meal plan

Give a man a fish and you feed him for a day.
Teach a man to fish and you feed him for a lifetime

CHINESE PROVERB

Whether it's a quick, casual one-dish meal (what I call 'one-pot cooking') or an elaborate banquet, when you plan your menu I recommend you first have some understanding of the traditional Indian meal. It's also good to have some idea of the philosophy behind it.

Fundamentals of the cuisine were formed over three centuries ago and the rules that guided it were based on an ancient theory on health called 'Ayurveda'. 'Ayur' is derived from the Sanskrit word meaning 'life' and 'veda' means knowledge.

According to the texts, food is not just about sustenance or enjoyment, but also about maintenance of long life through the understanding of one's mind, body and soul. They name three primary life forces in the human body called 'dosha', which correspond to the three primary elements of air, fire and water. Our bodies contain different balances of these elements and so react differently to tastes, ingredients and combinations of food. The most important factor guiding a meal is the composition and balance of the consumer's dosha.

The properties of food are also viewed slightly differently than in Western food science. For example, using vegetable oil instead of dairy fats or ghee (clarified butter) does not just lower the cholesterol, but has a totally different effect on the body. Ghee is seen as cooling to the body, whereas oil heats it.

These days there is a common belief that healthy eating is all about fresh vegetarian meals, and that flesh has negative emotions and the force of violence attached to it, which is out of keeping with 'purity'. However, in Ayurveda the eating of fish or meat is not discouraged, in fact it is recommended.

A regular meal planned for an Indian household is a complex matter with several factors guiding it. The meals are not served up in courses such as appetisers, entrées or mains. Commonly a meal plate is known to everyone as a 'thali', which literally means 'plate'. Now, whether this plate is made of steel, silver, bone china or a banana leaf (as in the south), it's the composition of what's on it that is important here.

Basically, the meal would consist of carbohydrate (rice or bread), protein (lentils, meat or fish), vegetables (leafy, starchy, seasonal), dairy (yoghurt relish, ghee), pickles (pungent taste), and salt (yes, a lot of places still do serve a pinch of salt on the plate!). So plan your menu choosing one item from each of these categories and present it in a pleasing way either as many small items or one big platter with several items like a thali.

(By the way, you'll notice I rarely mention 'curry' in this book. This is not because the word is not used in India, but because its meaning has become so misused and generalised that I would rather leave it out altogether!)

beverages

An Indian meal is not complete without an accompanying beverage. Fresh water served at room temperature is a natural complement to most Indian fare and a healthy way to finish. There are also a number of beverages unique to the sub-continent that are designed to go with food. 'Panna' (green mango drink), 'lassi' (yoghurt drink), 'jal jeera' (cumin-flavoured beverage) and 'nimboo sherbet' (fresh lemonade) are some of the more common non-alcoholic choices.

Surprisingly, in Ayurveda consuming alcohol is not forbidden. On the contrary, some texts list several alcoholic drinks that strengthen the body, help digestion and promote rest after a meal.

The Moghuls and Nizams of yesteryear frequently entertained with wines in their grand courtroom banquets and since the 1980s India has produced, consumed and exported a wide variety of good-quality wine. The notion that spicy Indian food and wine don't work together is indeed just another myth.

Syrupy Gewurztraminer is a favourite with Indian food because it has a sweetness that can stand up to heat and complex seasoning. However, I feel the crisp, clean, easy-drinking modern wines are most appropriate. 'Shorshe bata maach' (East Indian fish in mustard sauce) served with a slightly chilled Tasmanian or New Zealand Pinot is sensational. And 'Karwari jheenga' (semolina crusted pan-fried green prawns) go particularly well with Sauvignon Blanc. For most 'medium spiced' dishes (a relative term, I know), like 'Butter chicken' or the well-known 'Chicken tikka masala', try Chenin Blanc.

As a general rule, simple reds rather than big complex wines complement Indian food. Try a Western Australian Shiraz with 'Nalli roganjosh' (Kashmiri lamb shanks) and a Cabernet Sauvignon with 'Raan-e-khyber' (braised whole leg of lamb). Most mild to medium dishes go well with Grenache.

More than just a starter, beer is excellent with a range of Indian meals and the traditional aperitifs like sherry, port or any other fortified wines are great with spicy food.

Qmin's 'Maharajah's Table' banquet and 'Beer and Curry' fare are immensely popular examples of the complementary interaction of food and beverages. Many of our guests are wine aficionados, and they are full of praise for our innovative food/wine combinations.

GLOSSARY

Achar: Pickle

Aloo: Potato

Anar dana: Pomegranate seeds

Asafoetida: 'Hing'. A stony resin with a pungent taste, used powdered.

Ash gourd: 'Bhopla'

Badi elaichi: Black cardamom. A large, fibrous black variety of cardamom.

Bhaji: Vegetables (in one Indian language).

Bhajjia: Vegetable fritters, a popular snack.

Bhunao: A method of cooking involving a combination of light stewing, sautéing and stir-frying. It is the process of cooking over medium to high heat, adding small quantities of liquid—water or yoghurt—and stirring constantly to prevent the ingredients from sticking.

Bindhi: Okra

Biryani: A rice casserole containing meat, poultry, seafood or vegetables.

Chaat: A North Indian salad-type snack—usually sweet and spicy, tossed with chutneys.

Chaat masala: Spice mix used predominantly in the north, available as proprietary mix at Indian groceries.

Daal (Dal/Dhal): Any kind of pulses: beans, peas or lentils.

Dry mango powder: 'Amchoor'

Dum: Literally means 'steam'. A cooking method of braising in a sealed pot.

Garam masala: A spice mix, whole or powdered (refer to recipe page 190).

Gosht: Meat

Jaggery or Gud: Solid molasses, resembles palm sugar.

Kaalia: Meats or vegetables cooked to retain some water or moisture in the sauce.

Kadi patta: Curry leaves

Kalonji: Onion seeds/nigella seeds. Small black seeds.

Kasuri methi: Dried fenugreek. Dried and powdered for use, highly fragrant. Originates from a place called 'Qasoor', now in Pakistan.

Khorma: Meats or vegetables braised in creamy sauce, reduced to remove all the moisture until the ghee separates from the sauce.

Masala: A blend of spices. Can be whole, or dry- or wet-ground. Gravy sauce base for a dish.

Methi: Fenugreek greens

Methi dana: Fenugreek seeds. Bitter if overcooked.

Pakora: A type of fritter dipped in a spicy chickpea batter.

Rai: Mustard seeds. Comes in at least three varieties: black, brown and yellow.

Shahi jeera: Black cumin. Literally, 'royal cumin'.

Tandoor: A deep clay oven, traditionally fired with charcoal.

Tandoori: Any item cooked in a tandoor.

Tikka: Small morsels, usually of meat or poultry but can be vegetable.

Vin d'alho: Meaning 'wine of garlic', a regional specialty of Goa. Better known as 'vindaloo'.

INDEX

Page numbers in *italics* denote illustrations. Page numbers followed by g indicate glossary items.